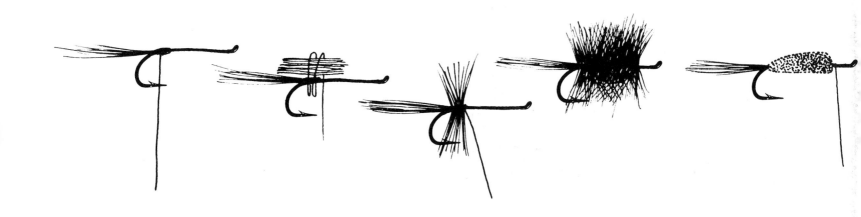

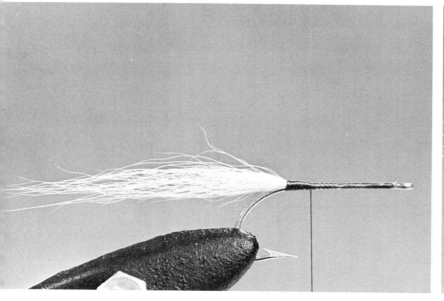

Dressing Flies for Fresh and Salt Water

Poul Jorgensen

ILLUSTRATIONS BY THE AUTHOR
PHOTOGRAPHS BY IRV SWOPE
Introduction by Charles K. Fox

Freshet Press
ROCKVILLE CENTER
NEW YORK

ISBN 088395-022-7

Library of Congress Catalog Card Number: 73-88891

Manufactured in the United States of America

Designed by Joan Stoliar

Most of our endeavors require a lot of practice before we become proficient, and fly-tying is no exception. You must practice to be even moderately good. I don't mean to imply that fish won't take a fly with too many windings of tying thread; but after a while the inexperienced tier will become more critical of his work and may not like what he sees.

When I look back to my early days of learning, I realize how extremely fortunate I was to have as my teacher and good friend the late William F. Blades. Bill was a master of his trade and is rated by many of us as the greatest fly-tier who ever lived. His book, Fishing Flies and Fly Tying, published in 1951 by the Stackpole and Heck Company, Harrisburg, Pennsylvania, is now a collectors' item.

During the years from 1955 to 1962 Bill and I became very close friends. We spent countless hours working at his fly-tying bench, practicing over and over again the varied manipulations of tying. "That's all it takes," said Bill. "Practice!"

Bill's death was a great loss to both those who were close to him and those throughout the world who knew him.

This book is my attempt to pass on some of the knowledge I acquired from the great master. I should like to be permitted to take up where he left off: "Practice, that's all it takes!"

With gratitude, and in appreciation for his friendship and loyalty, I dedicate this book to the memory of the late William F. Blades.

ACKNOWLEDGMENTS

I wish to thank all the fly fishers who have sent their favorite flies and patterns to me and allowed me to include them in the book. Credit is given with the individual dressings.

Special thanks are due to Irv Swope of Frederick, Maryland, for his patience and good humor while taking the many fine photographs. Without his talent and know-how they would not have been possible.

And to someone who shared in the labors on the book and offered untiring encouragement when needed, my devoted thanks—to Nancy.

CONTENTS

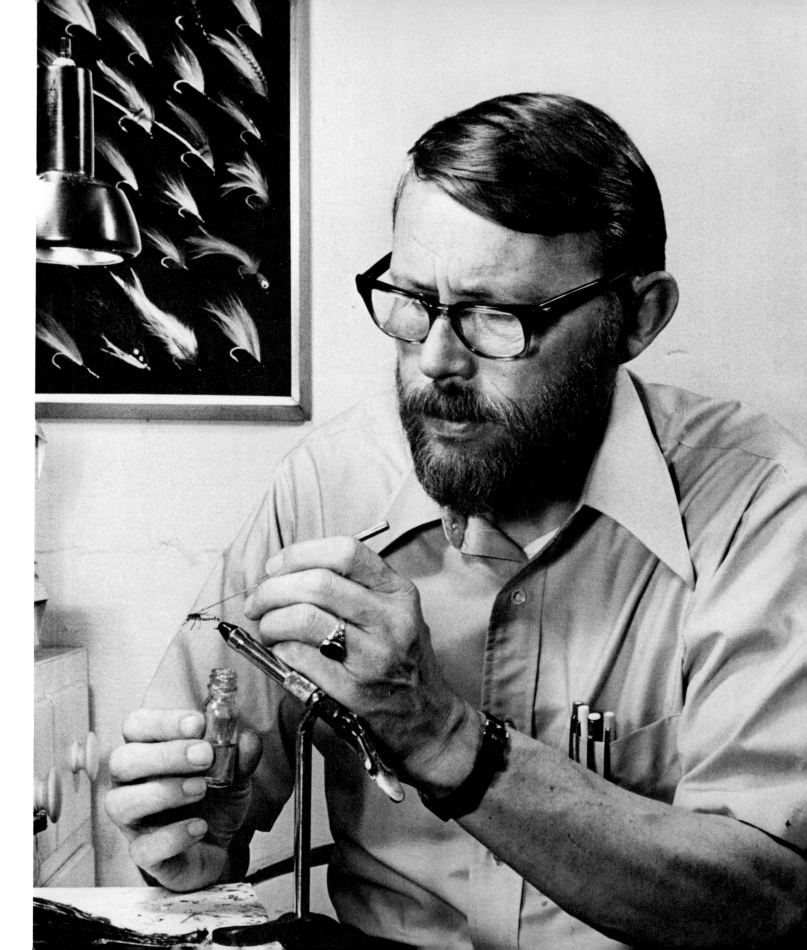

INTRODUCTION

As a professional fly-tier Poul Jorgensen has distinguished himself by his innovative methods. But his story really begins with the late William F. Blades. Bill Blades was an Englishman, transplanted to the Mid-West, where he taught fly-tying to private classes and to veterans at hospitals. It happened to be my role to edit the revision of his great work, "Fishing Flies and Fly Tying," now out of print because of complications with the rights to the beautiful color prints therein. I came to know him well enough to realize that to him the tying of each fly was an adventure and he liked to tie them better than fish with them. Two renowned pupils were the product of his fly-tying school. One is Ernie Schweibert, who as a boy wonder, tied flies on TV shows as the instructor looked on. The other is Bill's close friend Poul Jorgensen, who tied with him and fished with him prior to his passing.

Poul and I first met on a trout stream, in fact in my own meadow along the Letort. Now and then we run into each other either by a stream or at a Trout Unlimited meeting. In like manner his photographer, Irv Swope, and I first came face to face each with fly rod in hand. Both of these enthusiasts are members of the Maryland angling school.

"Dressing Flies for Fresh and Salt Water" enumerates the tools of the trade, the materials involved in dressing all types of flies and their specialized assembly. Good illustrations abound, along with the specifications of patterns.

A magician with fur, feathers, tinsel, and steel, Poul Jorgensen is the one to take the beginner by the hand and lead him down the road to the joy and satisfaction of taking fish on one's own handmade product. He is the one, too, over whose shoulder the old hand should look in order to learn more about the attractors and the deceivers and some refinements in their assembly.

It is fitting and proper that the out-of-print book of the old master be supplanted by a comparable work of his prize pupil. "Dressing Flies for Fresh and Salt Water" is a worthy contribution to any angler's library, even if he never expects to tie a fly. This well-illustrated writing demonstrates that in Poul Jorgensen we have a fly-tier's fly-tier.

Charles K. Fox

HOOK PARTS

A. SHANK
B. BEND
C. BARB
D. POINT
E. GAP
F. EYE

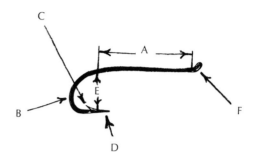

1

FLY-TYING HOOKS AND THEIR CHARACTERISTICS

Although the method of catching fish with a hook and line has been known to man for thousands of years, and modern methods of hook manufacture were known by the end of the fourteenth century, the hook-making industry did not begin until the middle of the seventeenth century, when English needlemakers incorporated hookmaking into their industry. Fish-hook manufacturing quickly spread to other European countries, particularly to Norway. Today Norway is the world's leading hook manufacturing country. Under the brand name of O. Mustad & Son, the Norwegians make a complete line of hooks, using only the finest tempered steel. Many of these hooks are designed specifically for fly-tying. Hooks for fly-tying are made in other countries, most notably England, but not all sizes of English hooks are readily available and distribution is to but a few supply houses in this country.

A selection of Mustad hooks will cover all your needs and enable you to tie all the flies presented in this book. The only hook I use other than the Mustad line is one called Wilson's Dry Salmon Hook. I recommend it highly for the purpose for which it was designed.

It is important that at the outset of your fly-tying practice you become thoroughly familiar with the many sizes and shapes of hooks you will be using.

The dry fly, an insect imitation, is designed to float on the surface of the water. Its floating ability depends on its design and on the materials used to tie it; therefore, for dry flies you should use the lightest hook available in the appropriate size.

Flies fished below the surface—nymphs, wet flies, and streamers—imitate underwater insects or bait fish and should be tied on heavier hooks in order to sink them to where the fish are feeding.

To aid in correctly identifying hooks, manufacturers use the code letter "X" in addition to size number and type. All manufacturers produce hooks in a standard diameter wire for each hook size, but many hooks are

FLY-TYING HOOKS

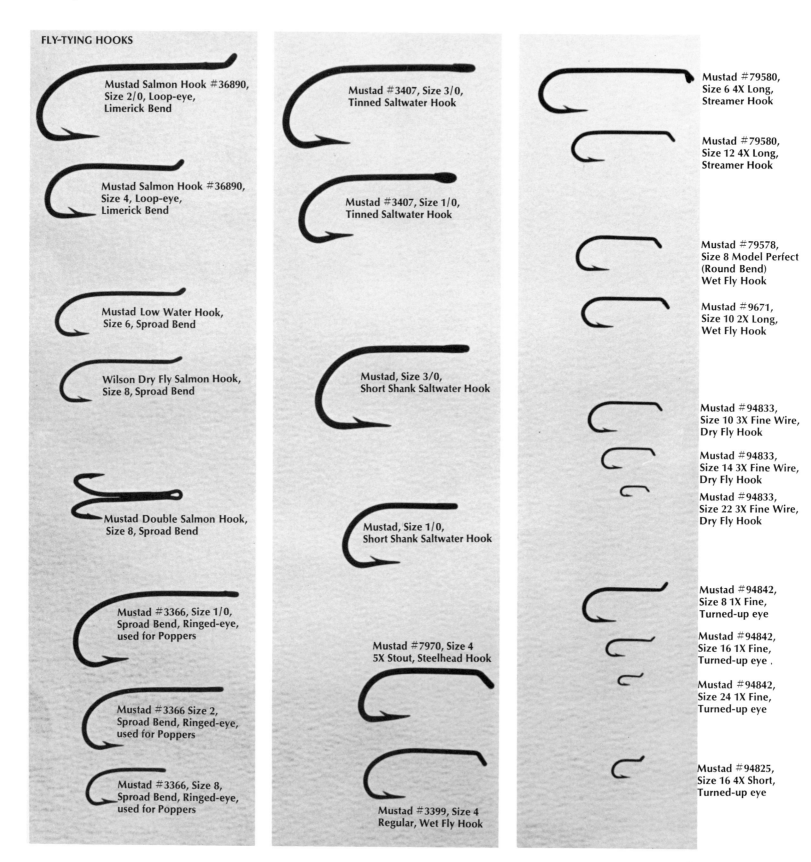

Mustad Salmon Hook #36890, Size 2/0, Loop-eye, Limerick Bend

Mustad Salmon Hook #36890, Size 4, Loop-eye, Limerick Bend

Mustad Low Water Hook, Size 6, Sproad Bend

Wilson Dry Fly Salmon Hook, Size 8, Sproad Bend

Mustad Double Salmon Hook, Size 8, Sproad Bend

Mustad #3366, Size 1/0, Sproad Bend, Ringed-eye, used for Poppers

Mustad #3366 Size 2, Sproad Bend, Ringed-eye, used for Poppers

Mustad #3366, Size 8, Sproad Bend, Ringed-eye, used for Poppers

Mustad #3407, Size 3/0, Tinned Saltwater Hook

Mustad #3407, Size 1/0, Tinned Saltwater Hook

Mustad, Size 3/0, Short Shank Saltwater Hook

Mustad, Size 1/0, Short Shank Saltwater Hook

Mustad #7970, Size 4 5X Stout, Steelhead Hook

Mustad #3399, Size 4 Regular, Wet Fly Hook

Mustad #79580, Size 6 4X Long, Streamer Hook

Mustad #79580, Size 12 4X Long, Streamer Hook

Mustad #79578, Size 8 Model Perfect (Round Bend) Wet Fly Hook

Mustad #9671, Size 10 2X Long, Wet Fly Hook

Mustad #94833, Size 10 3X Fine Wire, Dry Fly Hook

Mustad #94833, Size 14 3X Fine Wire, Dry Fly Hook

Mustad #94833, Size 22 3X Fine Wire, Dry Fly Hook

Mustad #94842, Size 8 1X Fine, Turned-up eye

Mustad #94842, Size 16 1X Fine, Turned-up eye .

Mustad #94842, Size 24 1X Fine, Turned-up eye

Mustad #94825, Size 16 4X Short, Turned-up eye

also made with wire that is either lighter or heavier than standard.

Wire for a dry-fly hook is smaller in diameter, and therefore lighter, than that for a wet-fly hook of the same size. For example, if a wet-fly hook size is designated as 1X, 2X, 3X, or 4X Stout, it means that the wire diameter used is equal to the standard or regular wire used for hooks one, two, three, or four sizes larger. Dry-fly hooks are marked 1X, 2X, and 3X Fine, meaning that the wire is the same as the standard wire for hooks one, two, and three sizes smaller.

Generally speaking, you will rarely need a hook heavier than 2X Stout. If additional weight is needed to sink the fly, I prefer to wrap the hook shank with lead wire before dressing. You may also apply strip lead to the leader.

Hook-length variations from standard are indicated as 1X to 8X Long and 1X to 5X Short. The same progressive method is used as for wire-diameter identification.

The position of the eye and the bend or shape of the hook is also important to the tier. "Up-eyed" hooks are often used for small dry flies to insure maximum hooking efficiency. I prefer "up-eyed" hooks for all my dry flies, but this is a personal preference. For wet flies and most fresh-water streamers, I use hooks with the eye turned down. I tie my salt-water flies on hooks with a "ringed" eye, which is parallel with the hook shank.

Salmon hooks are considerably stronger than average hooks, since extra-heavy wire is used in their construction. They are usually 1X Long. "Low-water salmon flies," however, are an exception; they are tied on finer wire, 2X Long. Salmon dry-fly hooks are also made with light wire, 1X Long.

Hooks for salt-water fishing must be stainless steel or tinned or nickel-plated to prevent rust and corrosion. (Stainless steel hooks don't rust when sharpened; plated hooks do.) Hooks for these large flies are made of heavy wire and usually range in size from 2 to 5/0, either Regular or 5X Short. Slightly larger or smaller hooks are occasionally used. Because of its lighter weight, the 5X Short is favored.

Some steelhead flies are dressed on hooks used for salt-water flies, usually size 1, 5X Short, with either ringed or turned-up eye. The short shank enables the fly-tier to dress a small fly on a wide-gap hook and thus increase his hooking efficiency. It is also possible to tie steelhead flies on small salmon hooks without detracting from the fly's appearance or efficiency.

The different bends are shown in Plate 1. The "Model Perfect," or "Round Bend," is the type most often used for dry flies. The "Sproat" bend is frequently used for streamers and wet flies. The "Limerick" bend is used almost exclusively for salmon flies, but it is also available on other types of hooks.

Hook sizes called for in this book should be considered a general guide only, for there can be many variations.

One final word of caution: hook manufacturers maintain high standards of quality control in production; nevertheless, most hooks are dull. Perhaps they leave the sharpening to the user. I take time to sharpen all of my hooks and advise that you do the same.

2

TOOLS

In fly-tying, as in most crafts, it pays to buy the best tools obtainable. There is no point in handicapping yourself by using inferior tools or fewer tools than are necessary to do the job properly.

Hackle Pliers

This tool is primarily used for winding hackle and body material. It can also serve as a weight when several types of fur dubbing are being spun. This technique is explained in Chapter 4 (Beginner's Tying Practice).

Thompson's nonskid pliers have round jaws fitted with rubber. They are excellent for most work. However, it is sometimes advisable to use a pair of very small English-type hackle pliers when tying flies smaller than size 20, as their narrow metal jaws can hold even the smallest hackle.

Vise

By far the most important fly-tying tool is the vise, which is used to hold the hook while the fly is being dressed. Take the time to select your vise carefully, for only a few of the many brands and models on the market are suitable for serious fly-tying. Don't make the same serious mistake I made while I was learning. I started out with an inferior vise that neither held the hook properly nor allowed for adjustment. That first vise of mine made tying a frustrating experience, rather than a pleasant and creative pastime.

I am now perfectly satisfied that I have the vise that meets the most exacting specifications. It is the Model A vise made by Thompson of Elgin, Illinois. I have used the Model A for years. It is made of the finest steel available, can be adjusted to hold hooks in sizes from 28 through 2/0, has an adjustable head that allows inspection of flies

from all sides, and can be adjusted in height to suit the tier by loosening a wing bolt on the table clamp. Thompson also makes the Model F vise, which is designed specifically for holding large hooks. If you intend to tie a substantial number of large flies, you might consider the Model F as a second vise.

Bobbin

Some of the bobbins on the market are too heavy to serve in at least one of the roles for which they were designed, namely, acting as a weight to hold the thread tight. Some of them are so heavy they will break thin tying thread. The main purpose of the bobbin, however, is to hold the spool while the thread is being used. The most widely used type consists of a tube with finely polished ends to prevent the thread from fraying and two spring steel arms with cone-shaped balls on the ends to hold the spool. Even the narrowest spools can be used in this type, since the pressure can be adjusted by bending the arms. Bobbins can be obtained from your local tackle dealer or from the Orvis Company.

Scissors

A pair of fine-pointed scissors is an absolute necessity for cutting hackle and other light material. They should be from three to four and a half inches long, with short, straight blades. The Surgeon's Iris Scissors available from Orvis in Manchester, Vermont, fit the bill. For heavier work, such as cutting wing feathers, deer bodyhair, and bucktail, it is not advisable to use your fine scissors, for they might be sprung. For coarse work I recommend a pair of heavy-duty scissors with the same over-all dimensions but with larger, sturdier blades.

Dubbing Needle (Bodkin)

The dubbing needle is used to spread fur dubbing evenly on the tying thread; to separate hackle fibers, wing-quill sections, etc.; and to apply head cement and lacquer.

Additional Tools

In addition to the specialized fly-tying tools, you'll also need an X-Acto saw and a long, thin rat-tail file for making balsa heads; several one-quarter-inch flat jeweler's files; sandpaper; nail clippers; needle-nose pliers; and tweezers.

Half-Hitch Tool

This tool is used for finishing off the heads on dry flies. It consists of a round plastic or aluminum rod four to five inches long and about the diameter of a pencil. The ends are tapered and have holes in them to accommodate the hook eye and fly head. Frequently, when the hackle is wound and tied off, several hackle fibers crowd the eye, making it difficult to finish the head. That's where the tool comes in handy.

To use the half-hitch tool (see drawing **3**) hold thread tight toward you; place one end of the tool on top of the thread about two inches from the hook eye; take two turns of thread around the tool about one inch from the end with the loose end of the thread, winding over and away from you. Continue to hold the thread tight and roll the tool with your fingers until the end reaches the eye. Then push the hole over the eye and up against the hackle. Finally, slide the windings onto the hook and pull them tight.

Half-hitch tools can be easily improvised from a ballpoint pen with the ink cartridge removed, or from a large wing-quill stem with a hole in the end.

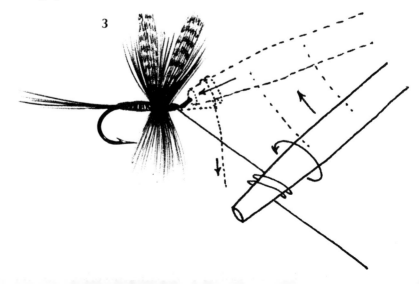

3
MATERIALS

Many people are somehow led to believe that before venturing into fly-tying one must first obtain feathers and fur from almost every bird and animal in existence. This is of course not true. In fact, some of my angling friends carry all their tying stuff in a small sewing box and are able to tie all the flies they need. It's undoubtedly true that some tiers make a point of owning everything listed in the suppliers' catalogues, but I suggest that quality be given priority over quantity. Many feathers that were used in the fly dressings originated many years ago are no longer obtainable, owing to import restrictions or laws protecting the various birds from which they were obtained. The jungle cock eye is one of the latest to be taken off of the suppliers' lists. Artificial or natural substitutes must now be used. Suitable substitutes are illustrated in the photographs in the chapter dealing with salmon flies.

Sundries _____

Wax. I prefer the non-sticky wax for extra waxing of tying thread when making fur dubbing. The sticky type is a bit messy, and I find no need for it.

Head Cement. A good clear head cement is applied to the fly head to prevent the tying thread from unraveling. I recommend the brands specifically made for fly-tying.

Tinting Cement. Reddish-brown, golden-tan, olive, or orange tinting cement, applied to a fly head formed with pale-yellow tying thread, is far superior to enamel or clear cement on tying thread of those same colors. Its translucency adds to the effectiveness of a well-tied dry fly. Unfortunately, it is not available commercially, so the fly-tier must make his own.

Dissolve a half teaspoon of the desired color fabric dye in one teaspoon of fine lacquer thinner and mix it with a half ounce of very stiff clear head cement. If darker shades are needed, leave the mixed tinting cement exposed over night; then add another batch of dye and thinner. Work with it until it is of the same consistency as ordinary clear head cement. It is then ready for use.

Rubber Cement. For application on wing feathers and fly bodies. This type of cement can be purchased in your local hardware store. It should be thinned before use with a special rubber-cement thinner.

Lacquer. For painting fly heads, balsa poppers, etc. A good lacquer can be obtained from your supplier in the following colors: black, white, yellow, orange, brown, red, green, and blue.

Balsa Filler. Before painting the balsa heads, I apply several coats of Aero-Gloss Balsa Filler. This is in liquid form and is easy to use.

Vinyl Cement. A fine liquid for application of feather and quill sections needing to be reenforced such as wings, etc.

Tying Thread _____

The brand of tying thread one chooses to use is a matter of personal preference, but it is advisable to obtain it from a reputable supplier who deals in silk and nylon thread specifically made for fly-tying. I have tried most of them over the years and have come to the conclusion that prewaxed 6/0 or 7/0 thread in various colors, 8/0 in black and white silk or nylon, nymph thread, and some heavy cotton or nylon thread in sizes A, B, C, and D will enable you to tie and fly regardless of size. Nymph thread is very useful for tying fresh- or salt-water streamers, as it ties flat like floss. I often form streamer bodies made entirely of nymph thread, and it makes a beautiful tapered body. It is also excellent for heads on larger flies for both fresh- and salt-water. Heavy cotton or nylon thread is used for deer-hair bodies and for wrapping hook shanks for balsa poppers. The prewaxed 6/0 and 7/0 and the 8/0 silk or nylon are for trout, salmon, and steelhead flies in any size.

Body Materials _____

Many of the body materials are available in the following colors:

White	Golden Olive	Red Spinner
Ash	Dark Olive	Ginger
Cream	Olive Dun	Brown
Straw	Green Drake	Fiery Brown
Yellow	Lime Green	Tan
Amber	Grannom Green	Cinnamon
Bright Yellow	Mole	Sienna
Naples Yellow	Gray	Maroon
Primrose	Dun	Claret
Lemon Yellow	Blue Dun (Slate)	Light Claret
Deep Yellow	Beige	Magenta
Orange	Buff	Purple
Burnt Orange	Fawn	Kingfisher
Dark Orange	Iron Blue	Pink
Hot Orange	Light Blue (Cambridge)	Hot Pink
Light Orange	Blue (Teal and Blue)	Silver
Gold	Dark Blue	Copper
Chartreuse	Medium Blue	Bronze
Bright Green	Silver Doctor Blue	Fluorescent White
Dark Green	Soldier Blue	Fluorescent Gray
Insect Green	Royal Blue	Fluorescent Yellow
Apple Green	Blue Green	Fluorescent Scarlet
Green Highlander	Turquoise	Fluorescent Blue
Worm Green	Charcoal Gray	Fluorescent Lime
Peacock Green	Black	Fluorescent Orange
Emerald Green	Red	Fluorescent Pink
Olive Green	Flame	
Medium Olive	Crimson	
Brown Olive	Scarlet	
Light Olive	Sherry Spinner	

It is quite likely that you will use only a few colors out of this large assortment, but the list can serve as a guide when you are copying particular insects or purchasing dyeing powder and materials. You can obtain complete color charts by writing to E. Veniard, Ltd., 138 Northwood Road, Thornton Heath, England CR4 8YG. By the way, ask for their catalogue, as they are one of the best suppliers of tying materials in the world.

Floss

This is a flat, narrow ribbonlike material made of silk or nylon fibers. The heavier single strand floss is used for large trout, steelhead, streamer, and salmon flies. The type that comes in several thin strands can be separated and used as single strands for small flies. Nylon nymph thread is very similar to floss but is much stronger and is often used for winding a tapered padding on the hook shank before a tinsel body is applied.

Tinsel

The French make excellent silver and gold tinsel that can be obtained from your supplier in narrow, medium, and wide stock.

Flat tinsel in those widths is used for ribbing and for dressing solid tinsel bodies. Flat embossed tinsel is used on many streamers. Its scale-like appearance makes it very effective. Oval tinsel is a very narrow, flat tinsel wound over a cotton core and flattened. It is used almost exclusively for ribbing and tags, particularly for salmon and steelhead flies. Round tinsel is made in the same manner and for the same purpose, but it is not flattened. Before tying in oval or round tinsel one must peel off some tinsel at the end of the strand, exposing the center core, so as to keep the tie-in position from being too bulky. In some cases I tie in the ribbing in front at the wing position and bind it down on the shank as the tying thread is taken to the rear. The body can then be dressed smoothly over it without bumps. The ribbing is then wound forward over the body. Thin solid wire in gold and silver is used on very small flies for ribbing, or simply spiraled over fragile body material for added strength.

Mylar Tubing

Braided mylar tubing in gold or silver is often used for bodies on larger streamer flies. It is available in three diameters: 1/16", 1/8", and 3/16". Most of the brands have a center core consisting of several strands of cotton thread. This thread is sometimes removed, so the tubing can be slipped on the hook shank and tied down front and rear. On some of the larger salt-water flies, the tubing is wound on the shank as tinsel to form the body. When this is done, the center core is always removed and the tubing is flattened before it is wound on. Mylar tubing is excellent for flashy extension bodies on salt-water flies. I have also used this type of body on large flies for northern pike and have found it to be extremely effective.

Mylar Sheet

This is an 8" by 10" sheet, silver on one side and gold on the other. When a smooth solid silver body is needed, as on the well-known Blonde series of salt-water flies, for example, just cut some strips of the desired width using a razor blade or a sharp penknife. These are then tied in and wound on in the same manner as flat tinsel. For best results I generally attach the strip in front, then wind it to the rear and forward again to the tie-in position, thus applying a double layer of mylar for a very smooth, even body.

Chenille

This material comes in many sizes and colors. At first sight it looks very much like a pipe cleaner. Its very translucent effect makes it suitable for streamer bodies and for many types of Wooly Worms, Caterpillars, etc. The fuzzy material is spun on a center core of silk or nylon, which can be exposed by peeling the fuzz off at the end before attaching the strand to the hook. Chenille is not suitable for dry flies, as it absorbs water very quickly.

Peacock Quill

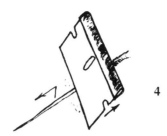

4

The two-toned quills for such flies as the Quill Gordon, the Ginger Quill, the Olive Quill, and others are found in the eyes of a peacock tail feather (see illustration **5**). To strip the metallic-looking fuzz off, lay the quill on a flat surface and hold it by the tip. Place a razor blade at a forty-five-degree angle, as shown in illustration **4** , and gently pull the herl out from under the blade, on which a slight pressure is applied. Repeat the procedure until all the fuzz is scraped off. I sometimes pull the quill out between my thumb and first finger and remove the fuzz with my thumbnail instead of a razor blade. Both methods work well when just a few quills are needed. If a substantial amount of flies is being dressed, one can strip the entire eye in just a few minutes by dropping it into a saucepan containing a solution of fifty-per-cent water and fifty-per-cent Clorox. This process will also bleach the quill a little on the light portion, though it will not affect the dark stripe. This makes the two-toned effect more pronounced. Don't leave it too long in the bleach, or it will become brittle. When the herl fuzz is dissolved, remove the eye with a pair of tweezers and rinse it in a solution of water and baking-soda. This counteracts the bleach, and the quill is ready for use. These quills can be dyed any color. They make fine-looking insect bodies. When quills are stripped with the bleach method they are often more brittle than those stripped with a razor blade or thumbnail and should be soaked in a glass of lukewarm water shortly before use.

The heavy herl on the upper part of the peacock tail feather (shown in illustration **5**) is used for herl bodies and herl segments on such flies as the Royal Coachman, Leadwing Coachman, etc. The rest of the quills on the feather can be stripped and used for darker fly bodies and ribbing.

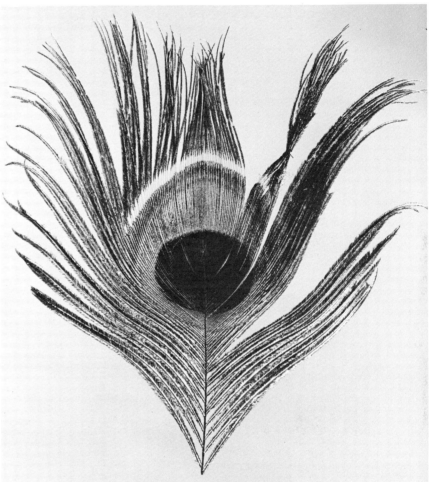

5   PEACOCK EYE
The divided portions on the right side of the eye indicate the location of herl for the
following uses:
LOWER RIGHT: Herl bodies and butts.
MIDDLE PORTION: Stripped and used for two-toned quill bodies.
UPPER PORTION: For quill bodies, as the middle ones.
The tip portion of this bunch is also used for wings on Streamers, etc.

23

Wool

Wool is best suited for flies fished below the surface, since it absorbs water very quickly. If used for dry flies, it must be carefully waterproofed. Most wool products can be used for fly-tying, but it is always best to buy wool from a fly-tying-materials house.

I recently needed a material to form a bulky tapered body on some nymphs. I came across just the thing quite by accident when looking through some gift wrappings left over from Christmas—a very heavy three-strand synthetic gift-wrapping yarn made by Hallmark. Most card shops carry it. I have since found many uses for it. It's particularly good when short butts or tapered bodies are needed. It's available in many colors and shades.

Raffia

This material, the fiber of certain African palm leaves, can be dyed any color desired. It is excellent for nymphs and mayfly bodies.

Before it can be used, it must be soaked in water for a few minutes. When it gets soft, it can be split lengthwise into strips. It should be kept moist while being wound on the hook, which is usually done over a tapered floss underbody.

Hackle Stems

Any large neck or saddle hackle with all the fibers pulled off makes a fine fly body with a very narrow two-toned segmented effect. The stems must be well soaked in water before they can be wound without splitting.

Moose Mane

The long moose-mane hair can be obtained in both light and dark shades. The two shades can be wound on the shank together for a two-toned body. Moose mane is

particularly useful for long mayfly bodies or for other flies for which peacock quill is too short. It can also be used for a small dark or light fly body.

Wing Quill Fibers

A single quill fiber from a wing feather of a goose, swan, condor, heron or any one of several other large birds can be a very effective body material for small flies. They are easily dyed any color. Tails from cock pheasants are also suitable for fly bodies. Ringneck, Armherst, and Silver pheasant tails are used.

Ostrich Herl

Although this type of herl is rarely used for whole bodies, it plays an important part in salmon-fly dressings, in which it is wound on the hook to form a butt or joint. In most cases it is used dyed black.

Horse Hair

Some very fine translucent fly bodies can be made with horse hair of different colors. The fly-tier should always have some available.

Deer Body Hair

This is the hollow hair from the hides of deer, caribou, and elk. It is used to make excellent fly bodies with a remarkable floating ability. The same hair is also used in some fly wings.

Balsa Wood

Lengths of balsa wood in many sizes can be obtained from any hobby shop. It is used to make the heads of various popping bugs.

Fur

Many animals supply the fly-tier with natural shades of fur which closely resemble the colors on the insects of importance to the angler. Pieces of skin from the following animals will give you most of the shades needed.

Red Fox. This is obtainable in gray, tan, fawn, and creamy white. The pinkish colored belly fur from the female red fox is much in demand for the well-known Hendrickson dry fly. Fox fur is very long, and in some instances it is gray at the base, cream in the middle, and tan at the tip end. Such fur can be cut in sections and is excellent for the spinning method used when dressing fur nymphs, spinners, and emerged duns.

Mink. Light brown, dark brown, reddish brown, rusty brown and tan furs are found on this animal. Most of the colors have a gray cast and make fine fly bodies.

Otter. A very fine-textured fur in cream and creamish gray. The guard hairs are often used for tails and wings on fur flies.

Opossum (Australian). This fur comes in black, gray, light tan, and creamy yellow. It is a rather short fur and is very good for spun dubbing.

Beaver. A nice brownish-grey to blue-grey shade.

Muskrat. The underfur from this animal is most widely used for such flies as the Blue Dun, Dark Cahill, and Dark Hendrickson patterns. It's a very nice blue or blue-gray shade.

Mole. This little animal has the bluest underfur obtainable. It's very fine for smaller flies.

Hare's Ears and Mask. These have rusty-brown to dark-gray underfur with speckled guard hairs. Its short texture makes it a little hard to dub unless the spinning method is used. For such flies as the Gold-Ribbed Hare's Ear and the body on some March Brown patterns, the guard hairs are generally left in the fur and are picked out as legs after the body is wound on.

Squirrel. Some parts of the skin are used to substitute for hare's ear, but it is more often used to supply the tier with fine tails.

Rabbit. Your supplier has small pieces or whole skins in many colors. I usually buy whole white skins from local surplus stores and cut them into pieces the size of a cigarette pack. I can then very economically dye the pieces any color I need.

Seal. Most seal fur is very coarse and should be applied on the hook with the spin-dubbing method. Its translucent appearance makes it one of the finest and most effective furs for bodies. It is used extensively on nymphs and salmon and steelhead flies. It is very easy to dye any color.

The animals I have mentioned are by no means the only ones whose pelts are useful to the fly tier but are merely the ones normally available from your supplier. Perhaps you will find colors or shades other than those I have mentioned on some of the animals named. They could vary. My hunting friend frequently gives me skins that are just as good as those from commercial dealers. If anyone dumps a jaguar, mountain lion, or raccoon on your doorstep, don't turn it down.

Spun Fur

Small cards of spun fur, usually in two strands, are made from the soft hair of the angora rabbit. These can be easily separated or pulled apart and made into fine dry-fly bodies. They are usually available in the same shades and colors as the furs previously mentioned.

Fur Mixing

Much as a painter mixes his paint, the fly-tier must know how to mix his fur to produce particular colors and shades. It is virtually impossible for anyone to set a rule for the quantity of different color furs needed to produce a certain shade, since the outcome depends entirely on the colors of the basic furs used. When possible, it is always best to secure a copy of the fly or a bit of blended fur to copy from. If a dressing calls for a creamish-tan fur body, it's fairly safe to assume that even amounts of cream and tan fur are mixed. If olive with a brownish cast is needed, the olive is chosen as the base color and brown is added in small quantities until the desired effect has been obtained.

The mixing procedure is quite simple. Just cut some fur from the skins and remove the guard hairs. Now mix the furs together with your fingers by pulling the fur apart and teasing and blending it until it is completely mixed.

An alternative and distinctly better way of mixing is to use an electric kitchen blender. This, however, may meet with some opposition from those members of the family who dislike fur in their orange juice. This form of fur mixing will be satisfactory for dubbing with the rolling and twisting method, but a different approach is needed when furs are to be mixed for use with the spin-dubbing method. (All dubbing methods are explained in Chapter Four.)

Fur Mixing for Spin Dubbing

In order to trim a fur body to the shape of the natural insect, the fur is applied on the hook with the spinning method and, except for dubbings involving seal fur, the furs are not mixed as in the previously described method. Mixing is accomplished by cutting thin layers of fur in the desired colors and placing one on top of the other before inserting them into the spinning loop. When spun, the thin fur layers intermix and the result is a very satisfactory blend. Like any other manipulation in fly-tying, this requires a little practice before one can select the proper amount of each fur needed for a particular piece of dubbing.

Wing Material

WING QUILL, TAIL FEATHER, AND HACKLE WINGS

The primary and secondary flight feathers from many of our domestic birds are used for wings on artificial fishing flies. To get the correct curvature, the tier must cut the wings from a left and a right wing feather. (See Photo **58** in Chapter Four under Quill Wings.) Matched feathers are available from your supplier, or you can buy the wings whole for a better selection.

The following descriptions may help the reader to identify the feathers when reading the fly dressings.

Duck. These flight feathers come in white, gray, and blue-gray (slate), depending on the species of duck from which they are taken. The blue secondary feathers with white tips are used on some flies. Duck quills are very good for medium-sized and small flies. The white feathers can be dyed any color.

Turkey. The wing quills are very large. Some have gray and white bars, others are brown or brown mottled. The tails are cinnamon or very dark brown, speckled with white tips. The smaller tail feathers are metallic blue-green with white tips. The brown-mottled wing quill is by far the most important to the tier.

Goose. The wing quills are dark gray or white and are excellent for large flies. The white feathers are available in many dyed colors.

Hen. The wing quills of hens vary in color, depending on the breed, but the most widely used are cinnamon, brown, and speckled brown.

Crow. All of the feathers are black. They are far superior to dyed feathers for fly patterns specifying black feathers.

Starling. The wing quills are very small, fine-textured, and dark gray. English starlings have small body feathers with white tips that can be used as whole wings or prepared and used as a jungle cock substitute (See Photo **200** and instructions on pg. *167*.)

Grouse and Partridge. The wing and tail feathers are cinnamon to brown, and gray speckled.

Peacock. The long tail feathers are very important to the fly tier. (See Photo **5** .) The green and metallic-green fibers on both the eyed feather and the long sword feather (sword feathers have no eye) are incorporated in many fly patterns by using a few strands as a topping or a large bunch for a whole wing. Good examples of such flies are the Moose River Streamer and the Sand Eel salt-water fly.

Marabou Plumage. These feathers are naturally white and are dyed many colors. Their soft and fluffy texture makes them very desirable for streamer wings. Cut a small bunch and tie them in the same manner as bucktail wings, or use whole feathers five to six inches long. An example of this last type of wing is found in the Apple Blossom salt-water fly.

Hackle. Many streamer flies are dressed with neck or saddle hackle for wings. The color needed is specified in the dressings.

FLANK AND BODY FEATHERS

Wood Duck and Mandarin Duck. Lemon colored with very fine dark bars, these feathers are among the most sought after by the tier. They are used for wings on Quill Gordons, Light Cahills, March Browns, Hendricksons, and many others. They are not always available, and dyed versions are often substituted. The black and white barred feathers from the same birds are mostly used for wings on wet flies, but they are now also being used as a substitute for jungle cock eyes. (See Photo **199** and instructions on pg. *166*.)

Teal. The feathers have the same texture as the wood duck but are white with heavy black bars. They are used in many trout and salmon patterns.

Mallard. The breast feathers are white with fine gray bars. The larger side feathers have more pronounced dark-gray bars on a light-gray base. They are called for in many trout-fly patterns. The larger feathers are used when tying the Darbee Crane Fly.

Silver Pheasant. The body feathers are silvery-white with irregular black bars. They are most often used on the sides of streamer wings.

Blue Kingfisher. The blue back feathers are used on the sides of some salmon-fly wings as shoulders.

Hair

Bucktail. The length of hair varies a great deal, and one should specify large, medium, or small tails when ordering. The tails are white with natural brown hair in the middle, and are easily dyed any color. I usually soak the whole tail in hot water and split it lengthwise. When it is split I run hot water on it from the base down. This makes the hair sit in a very nice curve, and a wing can be cut from the edge of the skin. To keep the hide from breaking, I apply a little hand lotion to it before it dries. The natural brown hair is used for tails and wings on streamers and large dry flies.

Polar Bear. When available, this translucent, shiny white material makes fine streamer wings and is often used on salmon and steelhead flies.

Black Bear. The hair on this animal can be used whenever a fly dressing calls for black hair.

Squirrel Tails. The white-tipped tail of the gray squirrel and the tails of red and brown squirrels are widely used. Many modern salmon flies are dressed with squirrel-tail wings.

Calf Tail. This short crinkled hair is used for hair wings on dry flies and streamers. Most of the shad flies I have seen are dressed with calf-tail wings, either natural white or dyed.

Tail Material

Most of the quills, tail feathers, flank feathers, and hair mentioned as wing materials can also be used for tails. In addition to those mentioned, the following should be added:

Amherst Pheasant. The neck feathers (tippets) are white with two heavy black bars. The tails are silvery white with black markings.

Golden Pheasant. The neck feathers (tippets) are yellowish orange and marked like the Amherst. The tails are tan and brown mottled. The golden-yellow crest is used for topping and tails on salmon flies.

Ring Neck Pheasant. The tails of the cocks are tannish brown with dark markings and pale purple edges.

The tails on dry flies are far more important than those on streamers and wet flies, since they to some extent determine the dry fly's ability to float in a proper manner. For this purpose, one must select the very stiff fibers found on large spade, neck, and throat hackles. When you buy a rooster neck you will rarely get the throat hackles with it. However, if there, they are located on the sides in the middle portion of the neck. The spade hackle is located on the saddle and is purchased separately.

The stiff guard hairs on beaver, muskrat, and other animal skins are excellent for tails on the Emerged Duns and Fur Spinners if attached in the proper manner. (See tying instructions in their Chapters.)

Wet-fly tails are not as critical, and it is best to use the fibers from either a hen hackle or a soft rooster hackle. Many of the birds mentioned previously have soft body feathers that can take the place of hen hackle.

Hackle

In the pioneering days of fly-tying in America the fly-tier had to raise his own roosters or wait until a neighbor's bird was old enough to be killed. Today one can order rooster or gamecock necks from a long list of suppliers.

The quality of the hackles used for floating the dry fly is very important, and the tier must take his time in studying the necks, as well as the individual hackles. A good dry-fly hackle is rather long and slim, with a minimum of web at the spine. The fibers should be shiny and even in length. They should stand straight out from the stem when the hackle is held by the tip and one's fingers are run down the center stem. (See Photo **42** in Chapter Four under Dry Fly Hackle.)

In time you will be able to spot a good dry-fly hackle just by looking at it. The location of the different sizes of hackle vary a great deal from neck to neck, but Photograph **6** indicates the approximate area where you should look.

The following neck hackles in their natural colors and shades are the most important.

White. These necks are usually not pure white. They often have a creamy shine on top. I prefer these cream-tinged hackles, as they are usually of a better grade than the pure-white ones.

Black. Natural black necks are very hard to get, and it is often necessary to use a brown neck that has been dyed black. Some blue-dun roosters have almost black necks, but these are generally of very poor dry-fly quality.

Cream. Cream necks are sometimes difficult to separate from white ones. They can best be described as being between white and very pale ginger. Art Flick, author of the *Streamside Guide to Naturals and Their Imitations,* recommends this shade for the Light Cahill.

Light Ginger. A pale tan shade.

Dark Ginger. This is a very light brown shade.

Natural Red. These necks are brown to reddish brown.

Coachman Brown. A flat brown to mahogany-colored neck that is specified for most of the coachman patterns.

Coch-y-Bondhu. A dark-brown hackle with black edges and tip.

6 ROOSTER NECK marked to indicate the approximate location of the various sizes of hackle.

LARGE

6-10

10-14

12-16

14-18

18-24

29

Furnace. These hackles are brown to dark brown with a very pronounced black center. They are very effective for streamer wings.

Badger. This is a white to cream hackle with a black center. Some hackles have a pale golden edge and black center and are sometimes referred to as golden badger, or badger variant.

Blue Dun. The natural necks are not only hard to get but also hard to describe correctly, as there are many different shades, from almost black to very pale gray and all the shades in between. The shades I use most frequently are light blue-gray, medium blue-gray, and a dark shade with a rusty shine, which is particularly good for Quill Gordons and other darker patterns. Fortunately there are some very good dyed necks available from some suppliers, and they are usually of better grade than the natural shades.

Grizzly. The necks come from the Plymouth Rock and are usually marked with white and black bars, though several other shades are available. These variant shades range from ginger and golden ginger to brown, or combinations thereof, all with the Plymouth Rock barred effect. They are strictly freaks and are referred to as red or ginger grizzly variants. They are very effective when used in some of the variant dry-fly patterns.

Chinchilla. These hackles are marked like the Plymouth Rock (Grizzly), but the bars are dun-gray and white.

Honey Dun. A pale honey color with brownish-gray center markings.

Dyed Necks. The suppliers generally have good quality dyed necks, not only as substitutes for the hard-to-get natural shades but also in many colors that do not occur naturally.

Saddle Hackle. These are available in most of the shades and colors mentioned in the listing of rooster or gamecock necks. Saddle hackles range from four to seven inches in length. Their structure makes them very

7

Saddle Hackle   Rooster Neck Hackle

effective for wings on streamers, poppers, and large salt-water flies. I sometimes use these hackles for bushy dry flies that require a lot of hackle, but because of the length of their fibers they are mostly suitable for flies of size 8 or larger. (See Photo **7**.)

Hen Hackle. The soft hen hackle is a lot easier to obtain than dry-fly hackle and is much preferred for wet flies. A suitable selection should include black, brown, ginger, blue dun, white, grizzly, and some variants.

Other Bird Hackles

Grouse. The body feathers are very effective as legs on nymphs and wet flies. They're dark brown with tan bars and spots. If this type of feather is to be wound as hackle, it is best to either double it or strip one side.

Partridge. Used for the same purpose as grouse hackle, these feathers are gray with fine brown markings.

Hen Neck Hackle   Spade Hackle   Grouse Body Feather

Guinea Hen. This body feather is very dark gray or black with white polka dots. It's used in the dressing of some salmon flies in its natural color or dyed blue.

Coot. The blue-gray body feathers on this bird are excellent substitutes for natural blue-dun hen.

Dyeing of Materials

Dyeing is necessary from time to time when a special color or shade of material is needed. I have found it particularly useful when tying salt-water flies with bucktail wings consisting of several shades of the same base color, for example, pale green, medium green, and dark green. The bucktail is ready to be dyed after being soaked well in hot water and washed free of grease with mild soapsuds.

Prepare the dye bath in a saucepan large enough to accommodate the material to be dyed. While the water is being brought to a boil, add a teaspoon of fabric dye for each pint of water and stir well to dissolve the powder. To set the color, I add one tablespoon of vinegar. Turn the heat down, and bring the water down to a simmer. Dip the bucktail in the dye bath and leave it in for a few minutes. Then take it out and rinse it in hot water. It should now be a very pale shade of the base color you are using. Bear in mind that the material is always a little darker when it is wet. If it needs more color, just put it back in the bath. The longer it is left, the darker it gets —up to a point. If it reaches maximum darkness and you want it darker still, additional dye powder is needed. For very dark colors, such as black, brown, and red, I often use the entire package of fabric dye.

Particular care should be taken when dyeing feathers. First they should be washed very carefully with soapsuds, since they are usually more greasy than hair, and second they definitely must not boil or come in contact with anything extremely hot, as this will spoil them.

When the material is dyed, rinse it in warm water and place it between paper towels to dry. For special shades, several colors of dye powder can be mixed together with very good results. This method of dyeing has worked well for me when using ordinary fabric dyes. Some suppliers of tying materials sell a dye powder which, according to them, was developed specifically for fly-tying. Before you use this, I suggest that you read the instructions on the package carefully, as they are different from those just given.

Storage of Material

To preserve your hackle necks, fur, hair, etc., keep them in closed containers with plenty of moth balls or moth crystals added. It is disheartening, to say the least, to find that a good natural blue-dun neck has been the main course at a moth dinner.

4

BEGINNER'S TYING PRACTICE

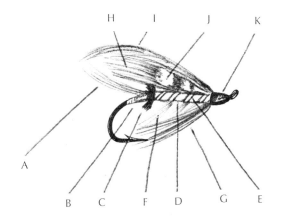

FLY PARTS
A. TAIL
B. TIP or TAG
C. BUTT
D. BODY
E. RIBBING
F. BODY HACKLE or PALMER HACKLE
G. HACKLE, THROAT or BEARD
H. WING
I. TOPPING
J. CHEEK, SHOULDER or SIDE
K. HEAD

Before we get down to the business of fly-dressing, it might be well to clear up any confusion as to what an artificial fly represents. Ever since man discovered that fish can be attracted by a few feathers properly arranged on a hook, he has involved himself in a study of the feeding habits and diets of fish. By careful selection of feathers and fur it became possible to produce fishing flies that in one way or another suggested the insects, bait fish, or other underwater life on which the fish were feeding. Early flies were designed to be fished below the surface and are known today as wet flies. Nymphs and Streamers, which are of much more recent development, are also fished wet. Streamers, which do not represent insects but are imitations of the various bait fish found in fishing waters, are not nearly as critical in their dressings as nymphs and wet flies. Although wet flies may sometimes be taken for small bait fish, they are meant to represent various forms of insect life, in many cases the nymphal stage of mayflies or stone flies. In other cases they were originated to imitate adult land or aquatic insects that for one reason or another become submerged. Nymphs, such as those presented in Chapter Seven (Fur Nymphs), are extremely important to the trout fisherman, since they represent the immature stage of mayflies. When ready to hatch the mayfly sheds its nymphal skin and becomes a dun, which is the form of the mayfly that is ordinarily represented by the dry fly. At the moment it appears, it is vulnerable to the hungry fish,

8

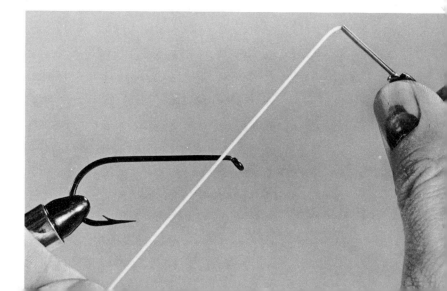

but many manage to escape and fly to safety. After its second and final transformation, it returns to the stream as a spinner to mate and lay its eggs, after which it dies.

The fly-tier should have some basic knowledge of entomology. It would be well for him to collect specimens whenever he goes fishing, as they are invaluable references when tying specific patterns. Above all, he must develop his tying skill through constant practice, which is what this chapter is all about. I am not concerned here with any specific pattern. This chapter will explain a series of steps which in the end will enable the beginner to assemble the wet- and dry-fly patterns that have been selected for this book, as well as many others.

Most of the tying methods I use are the ones that I learned from Bill Blades, so naturally they reflect the old master's techniques, though modernization of American fly-dressing has added tools and procedures that were rarely used in Bill's tying days.

Getting Started

The first, and most important, consideration when setting up shop is the vise. I hope you have selected the very best one you can afford.

Clamp your vise on a table or board in front of you and adjust it to a comfortable height with the jaws pointing to your right. To ease the strain on your eyes and make working conditions more efficient, you should have good over-all room lighting and a high-intensity lamp to illuminate your immediate work area. (See Photo **2** .)

Place a hook, let's say a size-10 Mustad #94840, in the vise with the shank parallel to the work surface. (Hook size isn't a major consideration, since this is practice, but a fairly large hook is easier for a beginner to handle.) Clamp it in tightly, burying just a small portion of the bend in the jaw as shown in Photo **8**. Hold the eye of the hook between your fingers and move it up and down. The hook must not move; you should feel only the spring in the steel. Place a spool of prewaxed tying thread of any color in your bobbin. Draw it through the tube and expose about six inches of thread. Hold the bobbin in one hand and the loose thread between the thumb and first finger of the other. Tighten the thread and lay it against the hook as shown in Photo **8**. The length of thread extended between the end of your bobbin and the thumb and first finger is about three inches. Hold the thread tight and take five or six turns with your bobbin hand in a clockwise direction, winding the thread on the hook over the end held by the other hand. The windings should be next to each other and wound toward the rear as shown in Photo **9**. The excess portion of thread held with your fingers should now be cut off close to the windings with your scissors. Continue winding the thread neatly down the hook shank to a position approximately above the hook point, as shown in Figure **10**.

The preceding practice is generally summed up as, "Place the hook in the vise and attach the tying thread."

9

10

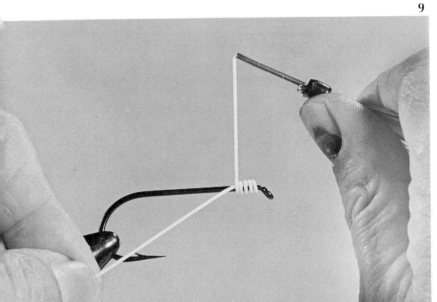

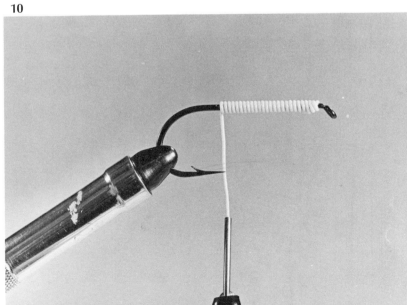

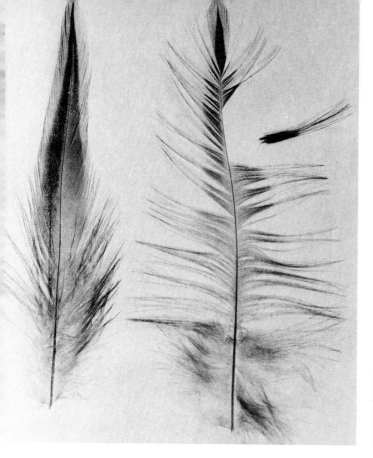
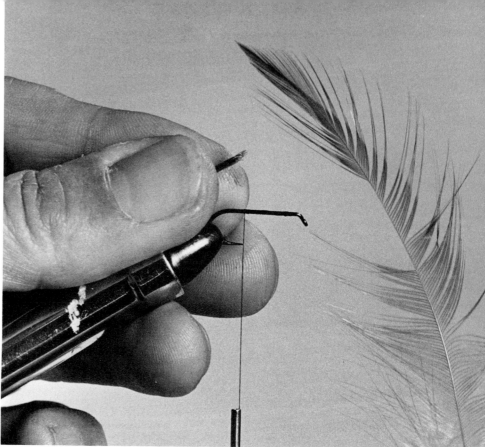

11 12

Tails

Although the material used for tails on artificial fishing flies may vary from pattern to pattern, the tying method remains the same and is applicable to both wet and dry flies.

Before continuing, you should thoroughly familiarize yourself with the information dealing with materials in Chapter Three, in which the difference between wet- and dry-fly tails is described.

Since you are practicing with no particular pattern in mind, you can use hackle fibers of any quality for the first tail preparation.

The tying thread having been attached, select a rooster neck or spade hackle with fibers long enough for the fly size you will dress. Hold the hackle by the tip and stroke it down the center stem a couple of times to make the fibers stand out a little. Gather six to eight fibers between

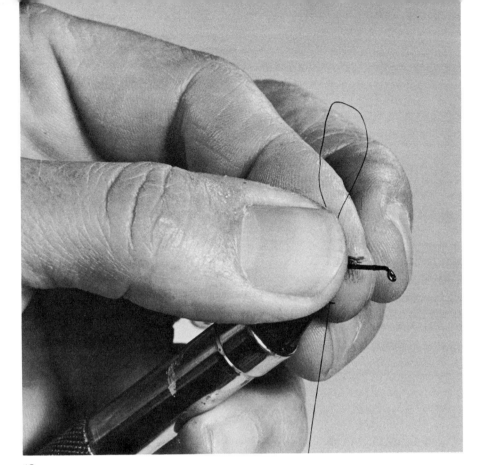

13

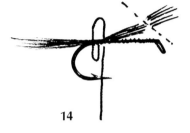

14

your fingers and hold them while cutting them from the stem with your scissors, as shown in Photo **11** (later you may learn to just pull them off). Regardless of which method you use, once the fibers are off the stem, don't let go of them. Work the fibers into a tight bunch between your thumb and first finger in such a way as to enable you to tie them in with the tips pointing toward the rear. At a point above the hook point, straddle the hook with your fingers as you lay the fibers down on top of the hook (see Photo **12**). Be sure you continue to hold the fibers tight between your fingers. Bring your tying thread straight up between your fingertips on the near side and hold it while bringing it over the top and pulling it straight down between your fingertips on the far side (see Photo **13**). A loop is thus formed over the material and the shank of the hook. Repeat the procedure a few more times, binding the fibers down on the shank. Wind

four or five extra turns of thread toward the rear around the material while moving it in a rocking motion with the fingertips to work the fibers into a compact bunch on top of the hook (see Drawing **14**). Now let the thread hang by the weight of your bobbin at the hook bend. Examine the results to make sure that the tail is straight. If it is slanting down, it was tied on too far back on the shank. This situation can be corrected on your next attempt.

For correct tail lengths, study the illustrations dealing with fly proportions at the end of this chapter, and by all means practice over and over again until the results are satisfactory.

The surplus butt ends are left as long as possible to serve as padding for the body. If they are excessively long, they may be cut with your scissors, but do not cut them shorter than one-third of the hook length from the eye.

Bodies_____

The body of a fly can be made of almost anything that can be wound on a hook. Some of the patterns I have seen over the years show evidence that this generality can be taken too far. Some materials lend themselves to use on fly bodies, while others are unsatisfactory. The list of suitable materials given in Chapter Three should be referred to frequently.

The Quill Body

The quill from a peacock eye makes a very effective two-toned fly body for both wet and dry flies. A picture of the peacock eye, showing the location of these quills together with stripping instructions, is given in Chapter Three.

On dry flies, the tail and wing are tied in before the quill is wound. On wet flies, however, the quill is wound on as soon as the tail is tied in.

Place a size-10 hook in the vise and attach the tying thread. Tie in six to eight blue-dun hackle fibers for the tail and let the thread hang at the bend. Select a two-toned quill that has been stripped of the herl. These quills are very fragile and should be handled carefully. I usually moisten the quill and make the first few windings with my fingers before grasping the end with the hackle pliers. Tie in the narrow end of the quill under the hook at the tail position with two turns of thread, as shown in Drawing **15**. Continue winding the thread to the right, stopping about 3/16″ from the eye and binding the butt end of the tail fibers and the short end of the quill down on the shank. Now wind the quill on the hook in a clockwise direction toward the eye, covering the tie-in windings with the first couple of turns and laying the succeeding turns perfectly side by side until the tie-off thread is reached. Take a couple of turns of thread to tie

off the quill. Cut off the surplus quill, if any, and apply a thin coat of clear head cement to the finished body. It should appear as in Drawing **16**.

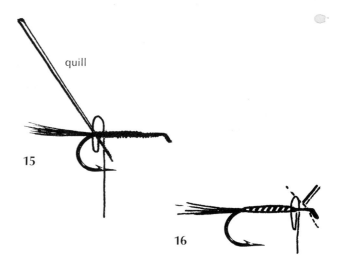

Since two-toned bodies are used for several of the better-known patterns, and the short length of a peacock quill limits its use to flies no larger than size 10, it might be well to mention two alternate construction methods.

The first uses two long moose-mane hairs, one dark and one light. They are tied in and wound on simultaneously. They make an attractive body that can be made as long as you wish.

The second method was explained by Art Flick, author of *The Streamside Guide*. He strips a large rooster-neck hackle of all its fibers and soaks the quill in water before winding it on the hook. For small flies, this makes excellent bodies with very narrow segmentations.

Floss and Tinsel Bodies

The Grizzly King and the Professor are two typical flies that use floss and tinsel together to form the body (see color plate). In most cases, a tapered body is formed with floss, after which the tinsel is spiraled over it. This makes the body more durable and creates the flashy segmentation generally referred to as ribbing.

Some English fly dressers insist that only five turns of tinsel be used to form the ribbing on any fly body. I must confess that I personally do not believe that six or seven turns make a fly less attractive, and besides, it has not, as far as I know, been established that fish can count.

For our practice, I have chosen the body of the well-known Grizzly King wet fly. This body is made of green floss with silver ribbing.

Place a size-10 Mustad #9671 hook in the vise and attach the tying thread. You can, if you wish, use size 6/0 black prewaxed tying thread. Select a narrow piece of flat silver tinsel four inches long and tie it on the shank above the barb with two or three turns of thread, holding it in the position shown in Drawing **17**. Take four or five close turns with the tinsel *to the rear* in a clockwise direction, going down the bend of the hook a short distance. Wind the tinsel back over the previous windings to one turn beyond the tie-in position. Tie it off with two turns of thread and let the long end of tinsel hang down to be used later for ribbing. Cut off the short surplus tinsel end with your scissors and let the thread hang down weighted by the bobbin, as shown in Drawing **18**. The little silver segment which is thus formed is referred to as the tag, or tip. It is used on many patterns, even when no ribbing is called for.

Prepare a red hackle-fiber tail and tie it in above the barb in the manner previously described. Wind the tying thread to the front, to about 3/16″ from the eye. Tie in a six-inch length of narrow green floss (single strand) with a couple of turns of thread as shown in Figure **19**, and let the thread hang. When attaching floss and other materials, I generally hold the material end between my thumb and first finger and tie it in using the same method as when attaching the tail. This prevents it from slipping.

Wind the floss down the shank till it reaches the tinsel tag and covers the original thread tie-in. Then wind the floss back to the tie-in position near the eye and tie it off with three or four turns of thread. Cut off the surplus floss. Grasp the tinsel with your fingers and spiral it up the floss body to the front and tie it off with your tying thread. Cut off the surplus tinsel and put a drop of clear cement on the thread windings. The body is now finished and should appear as in Drawing **20**.

When using floss, take care not to twist or spin it. If you do not keep it rather flat, you will not be able to make a tapered body.

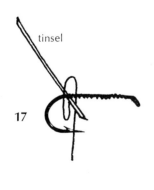
17

tinsel

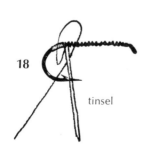
18

tinsel

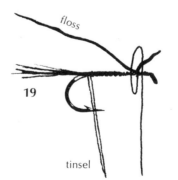
19

floss

tinsel

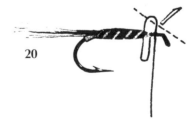
20

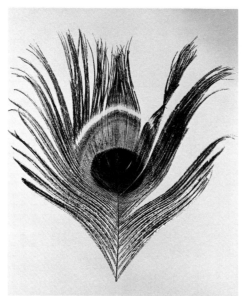

21 22

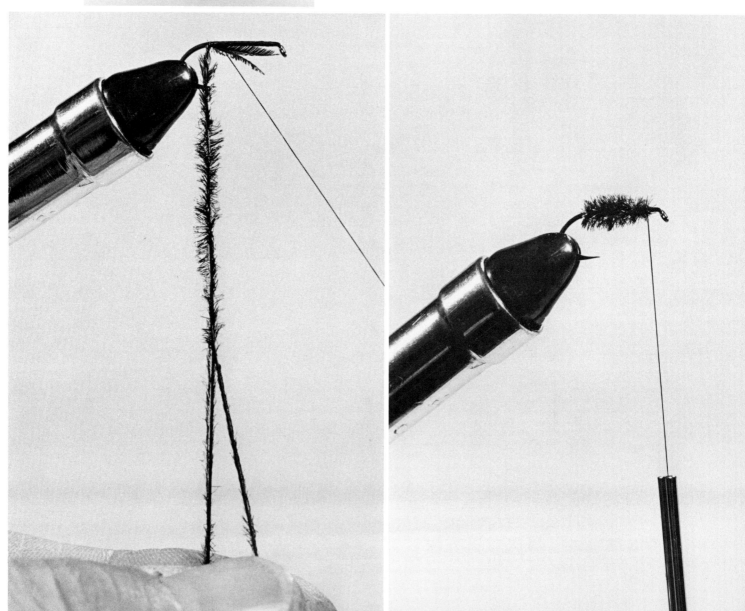

38

Herl Bodies

Peacock-herl bodies are very much in evidence on such flies as the Leadwing Coachman, Royal Coachman, and other important patterns. The thick herl for this purpose is located in the upper end of the feather near the eye as shown in Photo **5** in Chapter Three.

To tie the solid herl body for a Leadwing Coachman, attach the tips of two full-length herls at the tail end. The excess tip ends are now cut and the tying thread wound forward to 3/16" from the eye. Now twist the herls lightly together and your fly should appear as in Photo **21**. With your fingers, wind the herls up the shank to the thread position and tie them off. To avoid winding over any of the herl fibers, it is good practice to brush the fibers back with your fingers before you make each turn. Cut off the excess material with your scissors, and the body is ready for wings and hackle. See Photo **22**.

The Royal Coachman's body consists of a small peacock-herl segment in the tail end and a similar one close to the wing position. The two segments are separated by a wide band of red silk floss. Attach the tail fibers in the manner previously explained and tie in the herl as for the Coachman, together with a five-inch length red floss. Twist the herl together and take four or five turns around the hook to form the first segment. Tie off the herl with a couple of turns of tying thread before winding the thread to a position one-third of the hook length from the eye, as seen in Drawing **23**. Grasp the end of the floss with your fingers and wind it on the hook, taking the first turn close to the herl segment and each succeeding turn wound closely forward over the long herl ends to the thread position, where the floss is tied off with a couple of turns of thread. See Drawing **24**. Now cut off the surplus floss, twist the herls together and wind the second segment. Tie it off and trim away the excess herl ends. The finished body appears as shown in Drawing **25**.

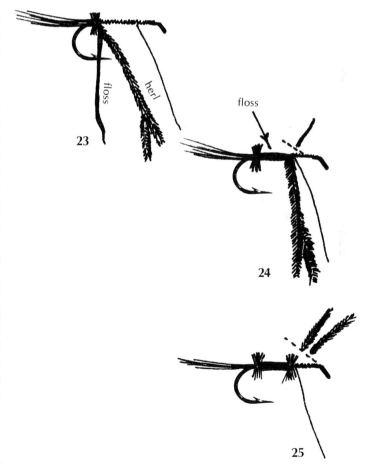

Fur Bodies (Dubbing) _____

Should I ever have to select one type of material and discard all the rest I would not hesitate to choose fur. Its uses in fly-tying are practically endless. Reading the chapters on Fur Nymphs, Emerged Duns, and Fur Spinners should convince you that it is the most desirable material of them all. In order to dress flies of this type, you must practice the various fur-preparation methods.

There are three practical methods of applying fur on the tying thread to form a fur body: rolling, twisting, and spinning. For each of the following practice sessions, you should prepare a size-10 hook with a tail tied in and the thread hanging by the bobbin from the tail position.

Rolling Method

Select a piece of muskrat skin and with your scissors cut off a small bunch of fur close to the hide. Hold it with your fingers and pull out the long guard hairs. This will leave the soft underfur, which is the portion to be used. (See Photo **26**.) Start pulling the fur bunch apart with your fingers, teasing and working it into a fluffy fur puff about an inch in diameter, as shown in Photo **27**. Grasp the bobbin and adjust the thread length between it and the hook to approximately four inches. Place the bobbin in the palm of your hand so that your fingers are free to hold the fur puff. Tease out a very small amount of fur with the fingers on the other hand. Tighten the thread and place the fur on the underside with your index finger about a half inch from the hook, holding it as shown in

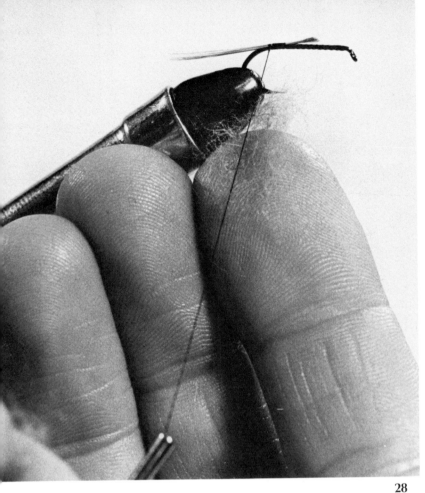
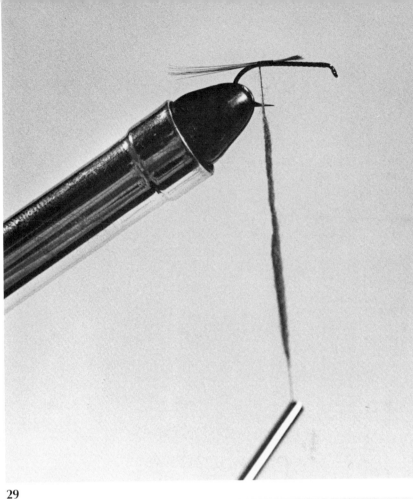

28   29

30

Photo **28**. Roll the fur and thread between your fingers *in one direction only*. At the end of the roll, release the pressure on your fingers and start a new roll. This will result in a thin, compact layer of fur around the thread. Continue to add more fur in the same manner, increasing the amount for each application and slightly overlapping the previous roll until the desired length of dubbing is made, which would be about two and a half inches for a size-10 hook. (See Photo **29**.) With more practice, you will soon be able to make a neatly tapered piece of dubbing of correct thickness and length for any size fly.

Wind the dubbing on the hook in a clockwise direction to the wing position 3/32″ from the eye. Tie off with two or three turns of thread and cut off the surplus. (See Photo **30**.)

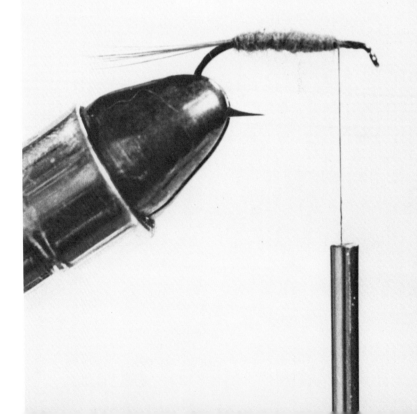

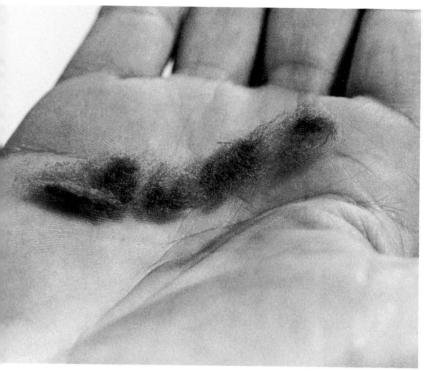 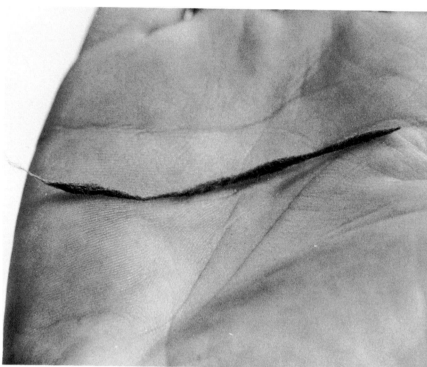

31   32

Twisting Method

With this method, the fur is not applied directly on the tying thread but on an auxiliary piece of thread about four inches long. This thread is formed at the tail position by doubling the tying thread back to its base and securing it with two or three turns around the shank. This double piece of thread will do nicely for flies size 10 or larger. For smaller sizes with thinner bodies, omit the doubling and simply tie in a single piece of thin thread.

Prepare a fluffy fur puff in exactly the same manner as described in the rolling method. Work it into a cylindrical bunch two inches long and about the diameter of a lead pencil and place it across the palm of your hand as shown in Photo **31**. Place your other hand on top of the fur and roll it between your palms in one direction. Continue rolling it until a thin, compact fur piece resembling an ordinary round toothpick is formed as in Photo **32**. Tie in the fur piece at the tail position. Bring the auxiliary thread piece alongside the fur. Grasp the fur and the thread in the jaws of the hackle pliers and let the pliers hang by the thread without any strain on the fur as in Photo **33**. Spin the pliers clockwise until the fur and thread are twisted together like a piece of rope. (Photo **34**.) Wind the twisted fur and thread on the hook as described the rolling method and tie off in front with three or four turns of thread. Let the surplus fur unwind before cutting it off, then take a couple of extra turns of thread.

A body formed using this method has the distinct segmented effect often used when tying nymphs, crickets, and grasshoppers. (See Photo **35**.) In fact, once you master this method and are able to produce very slim, tapered dubbing, you may choose to use it instead of the popular rolling method for all your ordinary dubbing work.

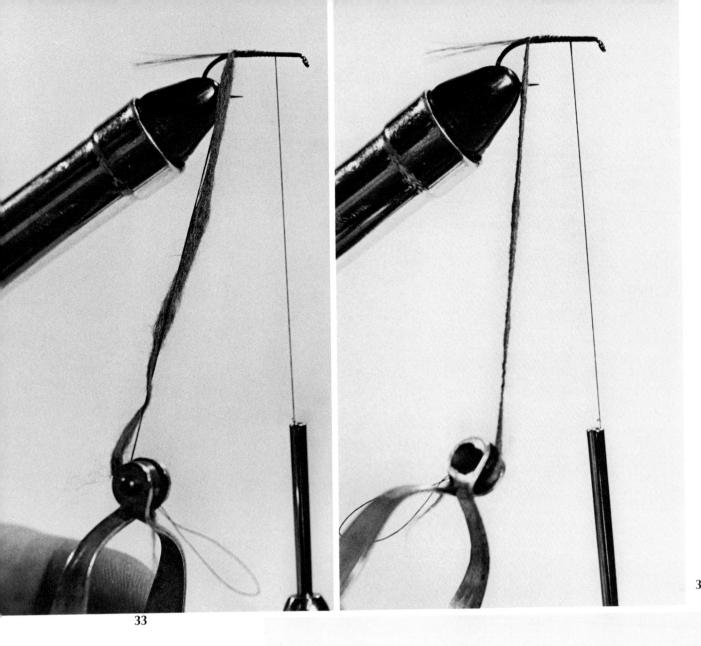

Spinning Method

Furs such as seal, hare's ear, and squirrel are difficult to work with because of their coarseness and short length. Nevertheless, they are among the most important furs when the fly-tier wishes to produce flies like the famous Gold-Ribbed Hare's Ear, the Fuzzy Nymphs, and bodies on many salmon and steelhead flies. That's when the spinning method comes into the picture.

First form a loop at the tail position with tying thread. To accomplish this, release about eight inches of tying thread between your bobbin and the hook. Wax the entire length heavily with beeswax. Hold the thread toward you with your index finger on top, three or four inches from the hook. Double the thread over your finger and back to its base. Secure the loop with three or four turns at that point before taking the thread forward to the wing position. (Photo **36**.) Expand the loop as much as possible and keep it open as it hangs at the tail position. Cut a bunch of fur from around the base of a hare's ear (avoid the really short fur on your first try) or a squirrel skin. Leave the guard hair in and hold the bunch between your thumb and first finger. Grasp the loop with the other hand and hold it tautly toward you, keeping it

36

37

38

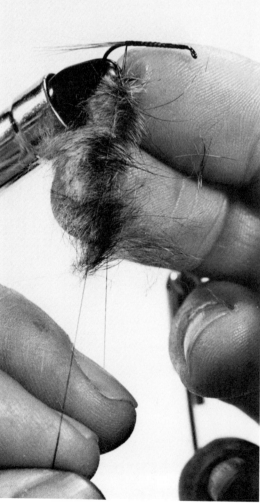
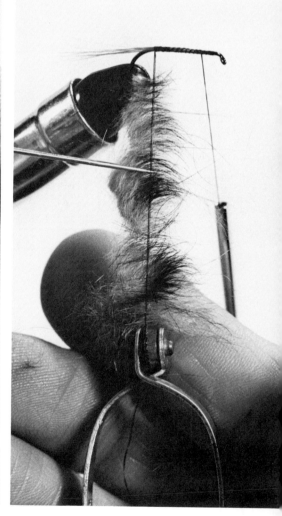

open with your index and middle fingers. Place the fur bunch in the loop close to the hook with the fibers at right angles to the thread, as shown in Photo **37**. Close the loop slowly by removing your fingers and pulling it tight with your thumb and index finger, thus trapping the fur between the two loop threads. Place your hackle pliers securely at the end of the closed loop and let the loop and pliers rest against your fingers. Spread the fur with your dubbing needle until a thin layer occupies about two inches of the loop (for a size-10 hook) as shown in Photo **38**. If additional fur is needed, open the loop carefully and insert it below the first bunch. Let the

loop hang by the hackle pliers and spin the loop rapidly until it looks like chenille. (See Photo **39**.) Wind the dubbing on the hook with the pliers in the usual manner, stroking the fibers back toward the rear at each turn to avoid winding over them. Tie-off at the wing position with three or four turns of thread and cut off the surplus. The result is a fuzzy, bulky-looking body that can be left as it is or trimmed to shape with your scissors. (See Photos **40** and **41**.)

If you want to succeed in tying the fur nymphs, emerged duns, and fur spinners presented in this book, the preceding dubbing method is the key to success.

39

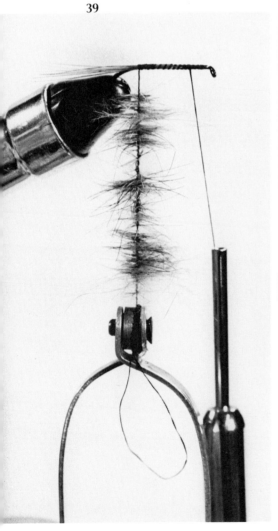

40

41

Applying the Hackle _____

The quality of hackle and the manner in which it should be prepared depends entirely on whether the fly is to be fished above or below the surface. Bear in mind that the hackle on wet flies is generally slanted back toward the rear, whereas the hackle on dry flies is wound on with the fibers at right angles to the hook.

Dry Fly Hackle (Vertical)

On dry flies, the hackle is the last item to be tied in. It takes a little patience to learn how to wind on the hackle, but you will soon get the hang of it.

Place a size-10 light-wire hook (for example, a Mustad #94840) in your vise and tie in the tail, body, and wings of your choice. (Tying in wings is discussed later in this chapter.) Let the tying thread hang by the bobbin immediately behind the wing.

Hackle can be a problem at first, and only experience can teach you to quickly identify the correct size for a particular hook. Meanwhile, study Photo **6** on page 29, which gives you the approximate locations on the hackle neck of the different sizes.

Choose two hackles located close to each other on the neck, so as to ensure uniformity of length and texture. Before pulling them off the skin, hold one hackle by the tip and gently stroke it down the center stem so the fibers stand out at an angle. The size hackle for a given hook size is determined by the length of the fibers in the middle of the top half of the hackle. In length, they should be from one and a half to two times the gap of the hook for which they are intended. Pull the two hackles off the skin and cut them in half, using only the top portion of each and discarding the rest. Pull a few fibers off the butt ends, exposing about 1/4" of the hackle stem, as shown in Photo **42**. Place one hackle on top of the other with their outer sides up and align the butt

42

ends. (*Note:* The outer side is the one facing you when you look at the neck.) Hold the hackles with your thumb and first finger as you place them behind the wing with the outer sides up and at the angle shown in Drawing **43**. To secure the stems and bind the ends down on the hook, take three or four turns of thread behind the wing and the same number in front. Cut off the surplus stems and let the thread hang midway between the hook eye and the wing. Grasp the tip end of the first hackle with your hackle pliers and hold it up with the fibers at right angles to the hook shank. Wind the hackle on the hook in a clockwise direction. Take the first two or three turns immediately behind the wing and the remainder in front, with the first turn close to the wing. Tie off with two or three turns of thread around the hackle stem. Cut off the surplus hackle close to the windings. (See Drawing **44**.)

Now, wind on the second hackle in the same manner. Take the first turn in back of the hackle already tied in and wind each succeeding turn through the other hackle toward the front. While doing this, move the hackle from side to side in a rocking motion to avoid winding the fibers down. Release any trapped fibers with your dubbing needle as you go along. Tie off the hackle in the same way as the first one, cut off the surplus, and push the front hackle windings back against the wing a little with your fingernails. Finish off with your half-hitch tool. (See Chapter Two for the use of the half-hitch tool.) Make a tapered head with tying thread and add several half-hitches to build up the fly head. Cut off the thread and apply a few drops of clear cement on the windings.

The finished fly should look like the one shown in Drawing **45**. Notice the appearance of the hackle fibers. If correctly applied, all the hackle fibers appear to be projecting from the base of the wing. This is by no means easy to accomplish, but therein lies the secret of a well-tied dry fly. It takes quite a lot of practice to apply hackle in a satisfactory manner.

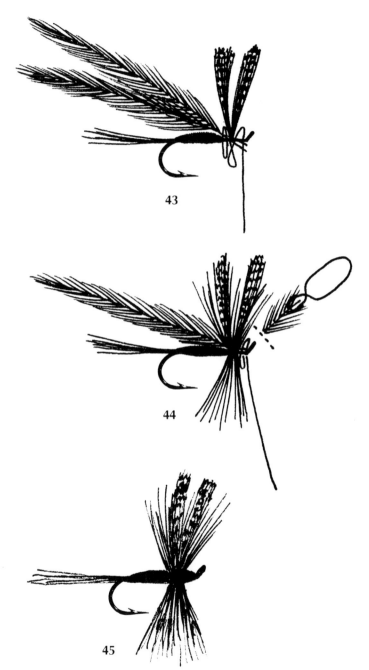

43

44

45

46

Dry Fly Parachute Hackle

This method of hackling differs from the others in that the hackle is applied in a horizontal position. It is used for spinners and for any other insect imitations the angler wishes to float *in* the surface film of the water.

To practice this method, place a size-10 light-wire hook in the vise and tie in a pair of spent wings fashioned from either hackle tips or duck flank feather. If you wish to finish some flies as you practice, the tail and body should be tied in before the hackle is added; otherwise the wings are all you need. Select a single rooster-neck or saddle hackle with fibers averaging the same length as the hook. Cut off and discard the lower part of the hackle and expose an inch of the center stem by cutting away the fibers on each side with your scissors. Leave some small stumps on the stem to prevent slipping when the hackle is tied in. (See Photo **46**.) Hold the hackle as shown in Drawing **47** with the underside of the hackle facing you, and secure it on the shank of the hook behind the wing with crisscross windings of thread so that the stem sits straight up. Clamp your pliers on the tip end of the hackle and start winding it clockwise and horizontally on the upright stem close to the hook. (See Drawing **48**.) Apply each winding under the previous one. After four or five turns, let the remaining hackle hang by the weight of your pliers on the near side of the hook. Hold up the fibers of the horizontal hackle with your fingers and take three or four turns of thread around the excess hackle tip and the shank. (See Drawing **49**.) Cut off the surplus and clamp your pliers on the vertical stem. Guide the stem down through the hackle fibers and let it hang by the pliers on the far side of the hook. Secure it on the shank with two or three turns of thread. Now push the stem down lightly from the top and pull down on it from below. Take some extra windings of thread around the stem before cutting off the surplus. Finish with half hitches or a whip-finishing knot and apply some clear cement on both the windings and the top center of the

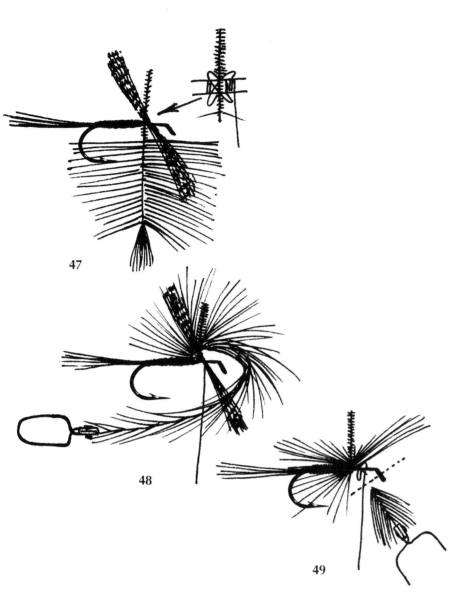

47

48

49

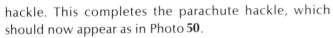

hackle. This completes the parachute hackle, which should now appear as in Photo **50**.

Parachute hackle can be applied on upright wing patterns by winding it directly onto the base of the wing. Simply tie in a single hackle on the hook shank close behind the wing; then wind it horizontally and tie it off as previously explained. Dry flies dressed in this fashion will float low on the surface film and imitate the freshly hatched mayfly duns.

50

Wet Fly Hackle

Wet-fly hackle is usually wound on before the wing is attached. However, as with all rules, there are exceptions, and there are some steelhead and hair-wing flies on which the wing is attached first and the hackle added in front. Whenever this is the case, it will be mentioned in the dressing.

Since it is desirable to use either soft, webby hackle from a hen or poor quality rooster neck, hackle selection is simplified and the supply is unlimited. This leaves only one major concern—size. For your practice sessions it is best to use a size-10 hook. When the tail and body are tied in let your tying thread hang directly in front of the body. Select the hackle and stroke it down the center stem until the fibers stand out a little. Determine the hackle size by the length of fibers in the middle portion. They should be as long as the distance between the eye and the point of the hook. Cut 1/4" of the tip portion away and clip off the fibers on each side 1/2" up the stem, leaving some short stumps to prevent slipping when the hackle is tied in. (See Prepared Hackle, Photo **51**.) Hold the hackle between your thumb and index finger with the first fibers held back as shown in Photo **52**. Secure it to the hook with four or five turns of thread and leave a bit on the stem between the windings and the first hackle fibers. Cut off the surplus stem and let the thread hang. Place your hackle pliers on the butt end of the hackle and raise the hackle to a ninety-degree angle from the body of the fly, with the fibers pointing crossways. Moisten your fingers and stroke back the fibers closest to the hook so all the fibers appear to extend out from one side of the stem. (See Drawing **53**.) Holding the fibers in this manner, start winding the hackle clockwise, releasing the fibers as you turn. Hold the hackle straight up after each winding and repeat the stroking-back procedure until three or four turns of hackle have been applied. As you complete the last turn—starting with the hackle pointing directly at you—follow the hackle with

51

your tying thread, winding the thread over the stem as you complete your last turn. Hold the excess hackle straight up, take three or four turns around the stem, and cut off the surplus. (See Drawing **54**.) Should any of the fibers flare forward, just fold them back with your fingers and wind on an extra turn of thread.

This hackle method is sometimes referred to as winding on a "hackle collar."

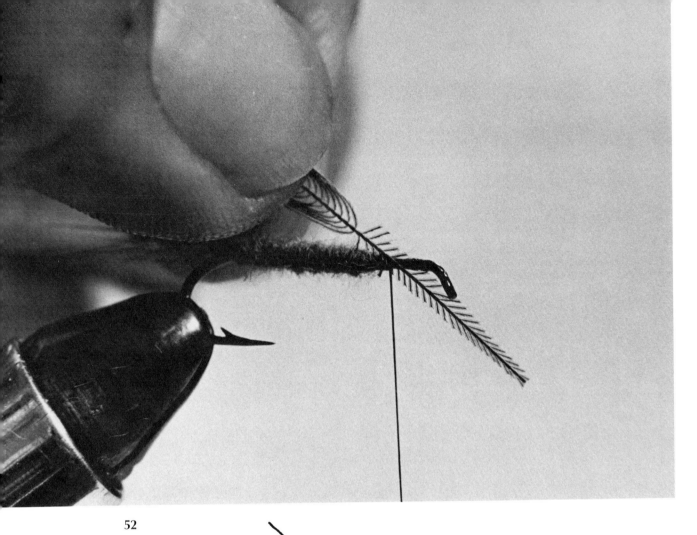

52

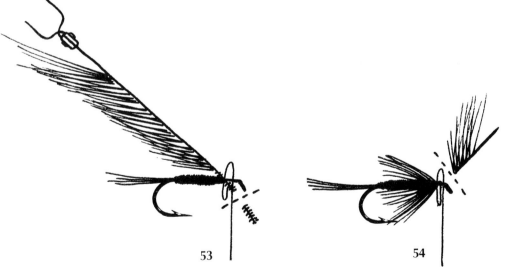

53   **54**

Palmer Hackle

When a fly is dressed with a hackle spiraled down the body it is referred to as palmer tied. Dry flies tied with this type of hackle in addition to the floating hackle have a very delicate descent to the water.

Palmer hackling is very simple to tie in. After attaching the tail and wing, prepare the body material to be wound on. Now select one or two dry-fly hackles of the proper size and prepare them for tying in by the tip in the same manner as a wet-fly hackle. Attach them at the tail position as in Drawing **55**. Finish the body and spiral the hackles over it to the front and tie off. (See Drawing **56**.) Cut the surplus and apply the floating hackle in the usual manner. Although the palmer hackle is prepared and tied in wet-fly style, it is wound on edge like a dry-fly hackle.

Photo **57** shows the Spirit of Pittsford Mills, a typical dry fly tied with palmer hackle. The Bivisible shown next to it represents a group of dry flies in which the body is omitted and replaced with several hackles closely wound palmer style up the hook shank, finishing off with a white hackle in front. Some fly-tiers wrap the shank of the hook with their favorite color floss before applying the hackle, while others tie in a thin silver or gold wire at the tail and wind it to the front through the hackle, in a direction opposite to the hackle, and tie it off. This makes the fly more durable, but it's anyone's guess whether it improves the fly's fish-getting potential. These flies are very popular because the white front hackle makes them easy to see when they are floated on a turbulent stream.

Palmer hackle is not restricted to dry flies. It is just as often used on wet flies for trout, salmon, and steelhead. The popular Woolly Worms, for instance, are palmer hackled.

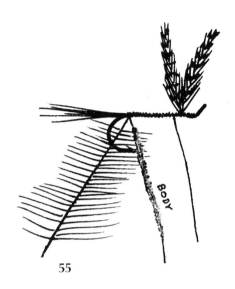

BODY

55

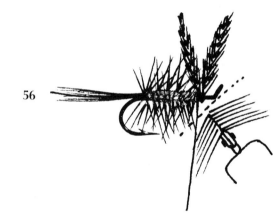

56

Wings

Most artificial flies are dressed with wings to closely resemble the natural insects. Wing material must be chosen very carefully. The angling fraternity has constantly tried to come up with new and better materials and tying methods, often only to go back to the old reliable ways that have been in use for many decades.

Quill Wings

Quill sections from the primary wing feathers of ducks, geese, swans, turkeys, and others are still high on the fly-tier's checklist for both dry and wet flies. One must select a feather from each wing of the bird to get the correct curvature. (See Photo **58**.) Insert your dubbing needle through the quill close to the stem and draw it out beyond the edge; repeat this step 1/8″ up the quill. Then cut the isolated section from the stem with your scissors. Do the same with the other quill. When taken from the same location on the stems, the pair of wing sections will be perfectly matched, as in Photo **59**.

The 1/8″-wide sections will do nicely for sizes 10, 12, and 14, but quill sections can, of course, be made as narrow or as wide as you choose for other fly sizes.

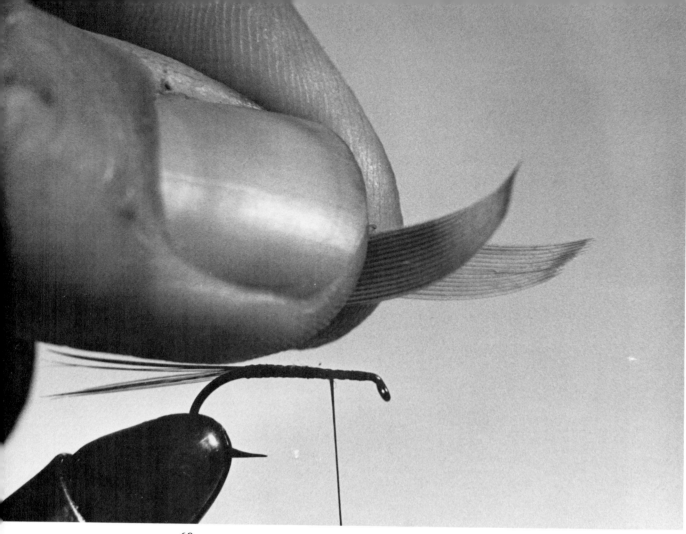

60

Although the quill sections can be used for both wet and dry flies the tying methods for the two types are different. When winging the dry fly, tie in the tail and wind the thread forward to 3/16″ from the eye. Place the quill sections back to back with the convex sides together. Hold them between your thumb and first finger as shown in Photo **60** with the approximate wing length exposed in front of your fingers. (See Fly Proportions, p. 87 for length.) Straddle the shank with your fingers as you place the wings on top of the hook. Fasten them with tying thread, using the same technique as for tying the tail. It is important to prevent the quill sections from folding when the first thread winding is pulled tight, so you must be sure to hold them very firmly between your fingers. When the wings are secured tightly on the hook, cut the excess butt ends to a taper, as shown in Drawing **61**. Lift the wings with your fingers and take three or four close turns in front of them. Make a horizontal loop around the wing base in a clockwise direction. Raise the wings to a ninety-degree angle from the shank while holding the thread tight toward the rear. (See Drawing **62**.) Tighten the thread until the wings sit in an upright position by themselves. Without slackening the thread, take a couple of turns around the shank, then crisscross it to form an X between the wings to hold them in a divided position. The tapered butt ends from the wings are now tied down on the shank where they will act as a tapered padding for the body.

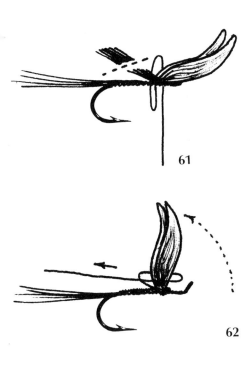

61

62

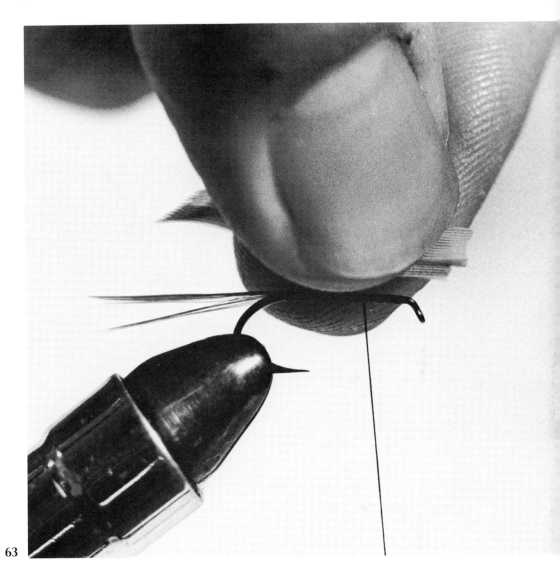

63

Wings on the wet fly are tied in after the body and hackle are wound on. The tying thread should hang down about 1/8" from the eye or there will not be enough room for the wing. The quill sections are placed together as before, but reversed, that is, curving in toward the middle rather than flared out as on the dry fly. Hold them by the butt ends with your fingers as shown in Photo **63**.(Note the length of the wing—it reaches to just beyond the hook bend.) Grasp the quill sections firmly with the thumb and index finger of your other hand and secure them tightly, using the tying technique previously explained. Cut off the surplus and wind the head. Finish off with half-hitches or a whip-finishing knot before applying clear head cement. The finished wet and dry flies (size 12 Blue Duns) will appear as shown in Photo **59**.

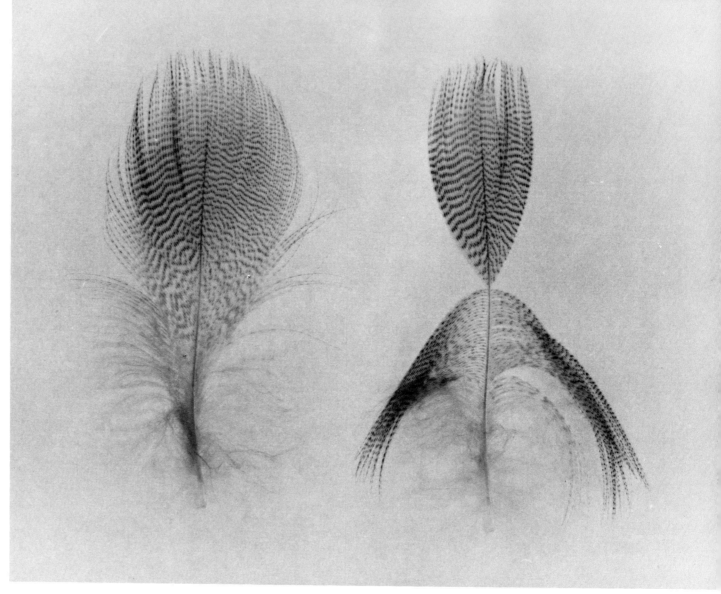

64

Flank Feather Wings

A list of the flank feathers most suitable for fly wings is given in Chapter Three. However, I suggest that the mallard flank feather be used for practice, while the precious wood duck be kept for some serious flies.

Select a medium-sized feather with fibers approximately equal in length on both sides of the stem, as shown in Photo **64**. Stroke down the fibers on both sides, then pull them off. The portion to be used is the tip section, which should be approximately 1" long. Now bunch the fibers between your thumb and first finger and attach

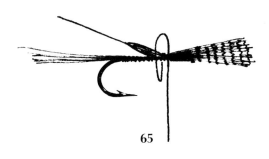

65

66

them on the hook shank in the same manner as the quill wing. (See Drawing **65**.)

For dry flies, the fiber bunch is divided into two equal parts and kept in an upright, divided position by tying thread crisscrossed to form an X between them to form two wings.

The wet-fly wing is not divided. Some tiers do not divide the dry-fly wing, but merely leave it upright. Inasmuch as some freshly emerged mayfly duns float for a short time on the water with their wings straight up, I suppose their method is justified. Photo **66** shows a wet and a dry fly fashioned with flank-feather wings.

59

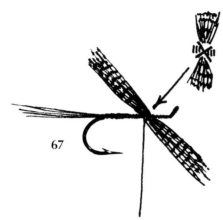

67

Spent Wings

Dry flies dressed with spent wings are known as spinners.
This is the last stage of a mayfly's life cycle. The flank
feathers from a duck are prepared and tied in as
previously explained for upright wings. The material is
first fastened on the hook, then worked into two
bunches of fibers which are tied down in a horizontal
position by crisscrossing the thread between the wings as
shown in Drawing **67**.

Hackle tips are used as wings on many spinner patterns. These are prepared by removing the fibers from
two dry-fly hackles. Leave sufficient fibers on the tip end
of the hackle stems to make a wing of the proper size.
(See Photo **68**.) Place the hackle tips back to back and
hold them firmly between your thumb and first finger
while tying them in securely as shown in Drawing **69**.
Now cut the surplus stem between the eye and the wing.
Work the hackle tips down to a horizontal position as
shown in Drawing **70** and secure them with X windings.

Hackle tips are often used in upright-wing patterns, in
which case they are fastened in the same manner but
secured in an upright and divided position like the quill
wing.

Another spent-wing method is explained in the tying
procedure for the Emerged Dun.

68

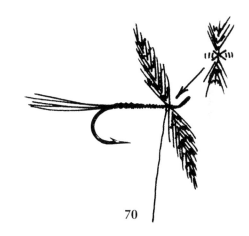

69

70

Hair Wings

The famed Wulff patterns, originated by Lee Wulff, are typical examples of hair-wing flies. White and natural-brown bucktail or any of the other hair types mentioned in Chapter Three are tied on the hook in the same basic manner as flank feathers.

Prepare a size-8 light-wire hook and let the thread hang from the shank 3/16″ from the eye. Cut a bunch of hair close to the skin, leaving it full length. (See Photo **71**.) Hold it with your fingers and remove the fuzz and short hair. Align the tips a little and tie it in as shown in Drawing **72**. Now divide the hair into two equal portions and crisscross your thread between them. Next, take a couple of turns around the base of one of the wings and raise it to a vertical position. (See Drawing **73**.) Tighten your thread toward the rear and take a couple of turns around the shank. Repeat the procedure with the other wing. Then build up a small bulk of thread in front of the wings and apply some clear cement on the windings. The finished wings, together with a finished Gray Wulff, are shown in Photo **74**.

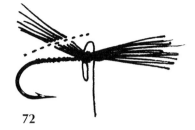

72

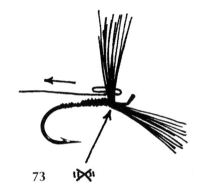

73

74

64 Hair is also used on wet flies. The tying method is the same as for flank feathers. However, the wing is generally tied in before the hackle is wound on, as in the case of the Orange Cole fly shown above in photo **75**.

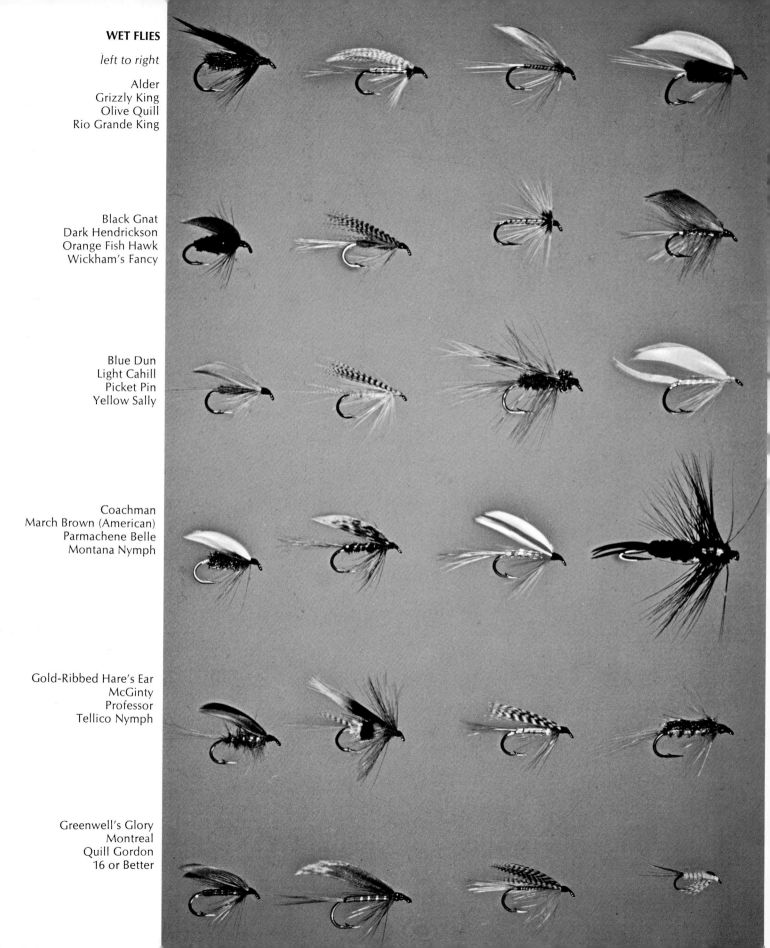

WET FLIES

left to right

Alder
Grizzly King
Olive Quill
Rio Grande King

Black Gnat
Dark Hendrickson
Orange Fish Hawk
Wickham's Fancy

Blue Dun
Light Cahill
Picket Pin
Yellow Sally

Coachman
March Brown (American)
Parmachene Belle
Montana Nymph

Gold-Ribbed Hare's Ear
McGinty
Professor
Tellico Nymph

Greenwell's Glory
Montreal
Quill Gordon
16 or Better

DRY FLIES

left to right

Adams
Grey Fox Variant
Quill Gordon

Badger Bivisible
Grey Wulff
Red Quill

Blue Dun
Hendrickson
Royal Wulff

Brown Olive
Light Cahill
Spirit of Pittsford Mills

Fox
March Brown
Sulphur Dun

STREAMERS AND BUCKTAILS

left to right

Badger Streamer
Esopus
Muddler Minnow

Black Ghost
Grey Ghost
Sabbeth Streamer

Black-Nose Dace
Hornberg
Spruce

Brown Hackle Streamer
Howard Special
Sunfish

Cock-A-Tough
Mickey Finn
Supervisor

Edson Light Tiger
Moose River
Yellow Marabou

Cut Wings

Perhaps the most natural-looking of all fly wings are those cut to shape from hackle or body feathers in shades closely matching the natural wings you are copying.

When selecting the two feathers, make sure they are fairly straight, of the same size, and have enough webbing so that you can cut the wing size you need at a point where the center stem is not too heavy. The photograph shows the preparation of a wing cut from a hen's neck feather. Start by cutting away the top portion at a point that will be the tip of the wing. Stroke down and pull off the fibers on the lower portion of the stem up to the point that will be the base of the wing. The fibers left on the stem should be sufficient for the size wing being made. Now trim the wing with your scissors to the shape shown in the photograph. I have lately employed a large toenail clipper available in any drugstore and quite frankly, it cuts a very neat wing and is now one of my favorite tools. The width is a matter of preference, but I have found that a width of a third of the hook length gives the wings a very natural appearance. When tied in, the wings are placed with the shiny sides together and attached to the hook in the same manner as the hackle-tip wings described previously. Cut wings are further explained in the chapter dealing with Cutwing Parachute Duns.

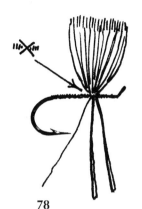

78

front view

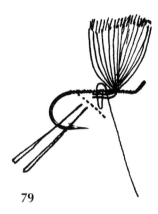

79

Fan Wings

The Fan Wing Royal Coachman is one of the most famous of all dry flies, and although it's not representative of any specific insect, the fish obviously approve of it. The wings are made of white breast feathers from a duck.

Select two feathers of the same size and make them the proper length by removing the excess material from the stem with your scissors, as shown in Photo 77. Place them back to back and hold them with your fingers while placing them at the usual tie-in position with the stems straddling the hook shank. Fasten them with several X windings, as shown in Drawing 78. Apply clear cement on the windings then tie the stems down on the shank behind the wing and cut the surplus. (See Drawing 79.) Take your time with fan wings. They must be straight and absolutely parallel or the fly will affect your casting and spin your leader.

Other Wings

Some wing types, such as those for bucktails, streamers, nymphs, poppers, and salt-water, salmon, and steelhead flies, are not explained here but will be described in detail in their respective chapters.

Winding the Head_____

Artificial flies can be true works of art. They deserve your full attention to all tying details, including the final stage—finishing the head.

Most fly heads are easily finished by winding over the

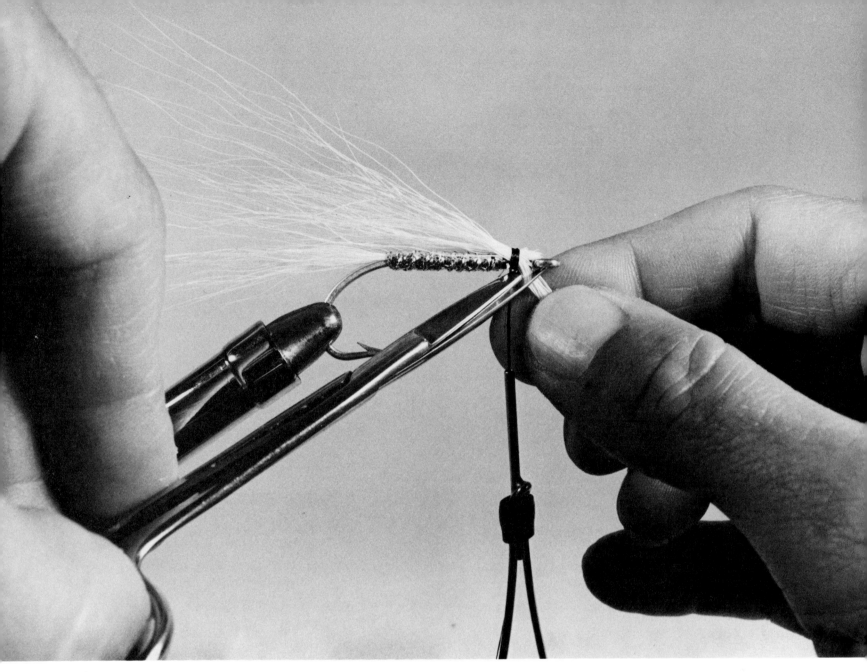

81

material ends with your tying thread and forming a small tapered head such as is shown in many of the photographs in this book. Where lots of heavy material is used, as with bucktails or multiwing salmon flies, a sizable bulk of material ends accumulates at the head. (See Photo **80**.) Use your scissors to clip such surplus ends to a taper just short of the hook eye, as shown in Photo **81**. Then form a tapered head with tying thread. For a super head on streamer flies, and on other large flies for that matter, tie in some nymph thread for your head windings. This will produce the smoothest fly head you ever saw.

69

Tying-Off

Once the head is wound, the thread must be secured in such a manner as to not unwind. There are three ways this can be accomplished: by using your half-hitch tool, which is the best method for smaller flies; by applying ordinary half-hitches; or by tying a whip-finishing knot.

The use of your half-hitch tool is explained in Chapter Two.

When the thread is tied off and cut close to the head, a generous amount of clear head cement is applied. The consistency of the cement should be such as to allow it to penetrate the thread windings and bind them

83

securely. After the cement is dry, a couple of thin coats of enamel can be added. Streamers and bucktails for both fresh- and salt-water are often fashioned with painted eyes, in which case the head must have a very smooth, even surface. To apply the eyes, choose two dowel sticks, one with a diameter equal to the size eye needed and the other with a smaller diameter for the center of the eye. Daub the paint on with the larger dowel first (see Photo **82**), followed by the smaller one for the center (see Photo **83**). These sticks must have smooth ends. For best results, dip the end so that you get only a drop of paint on it, then daub it lightly onto the head.

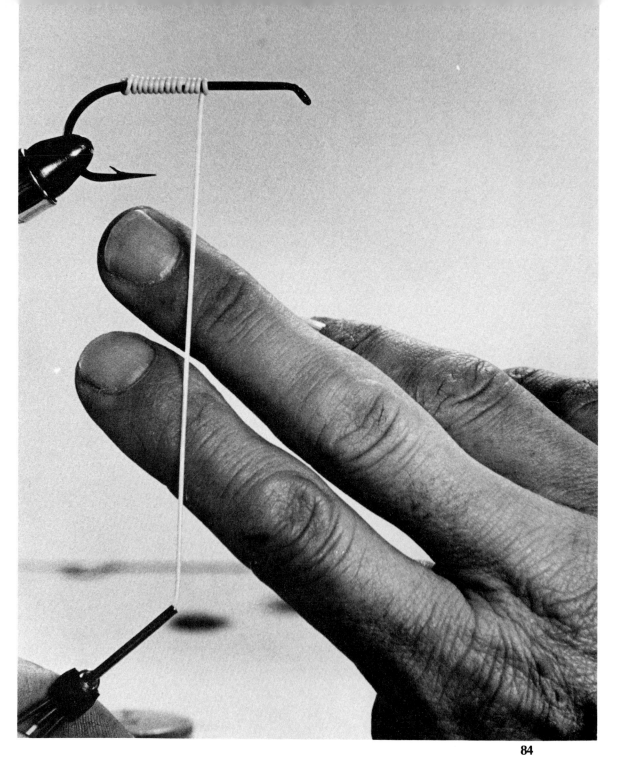

84

THE WHIP FINISH

Hold the tying thread tight toward you and place index and middle finger underneath close together.

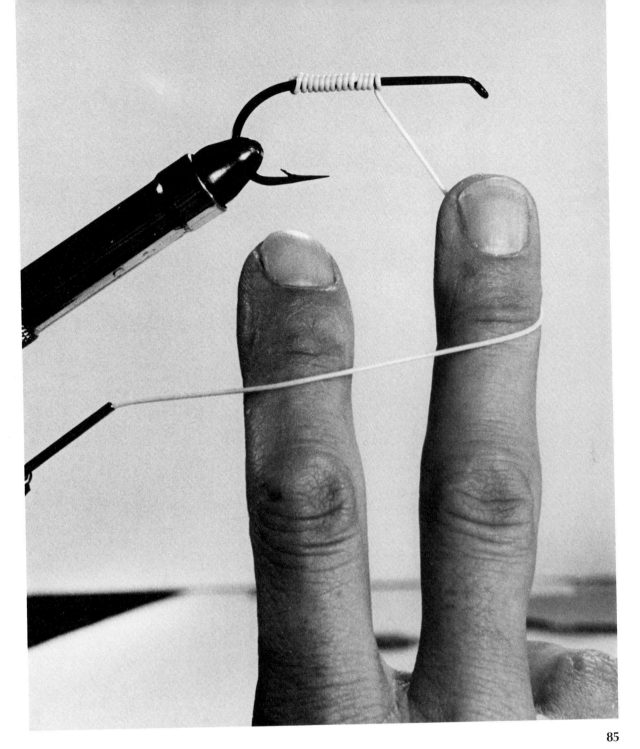

85

Separate the fingers while twisting the thread on the middle finger.

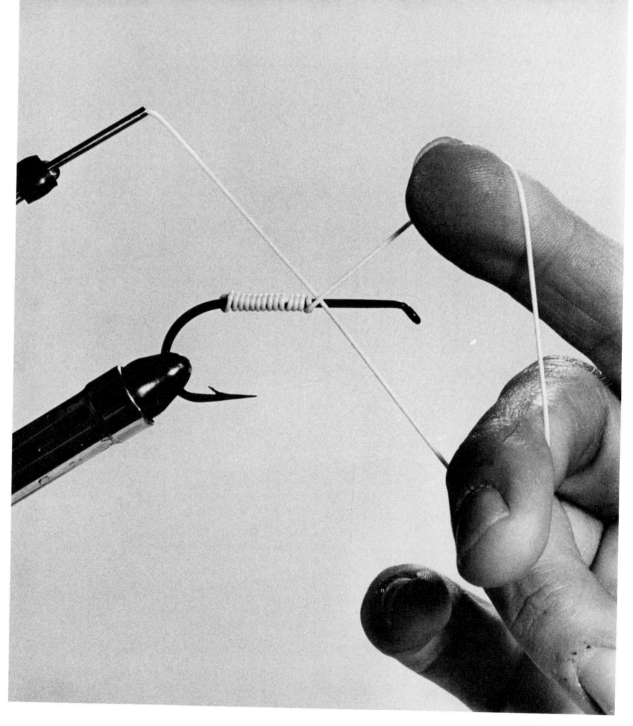

86

Twist your hand clockwise, thus forming a loop. Continue twisting until loop appears as seen in the Photo. Hold loop open with your index and middle finger.

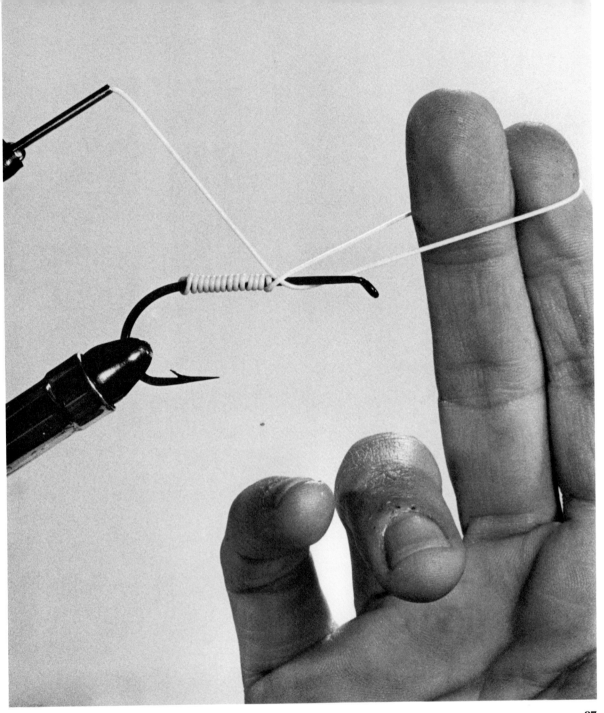

Move loop back, with upper part over the hook and lower part under. Move the middle finger close to index finger and hold the thread as seen.

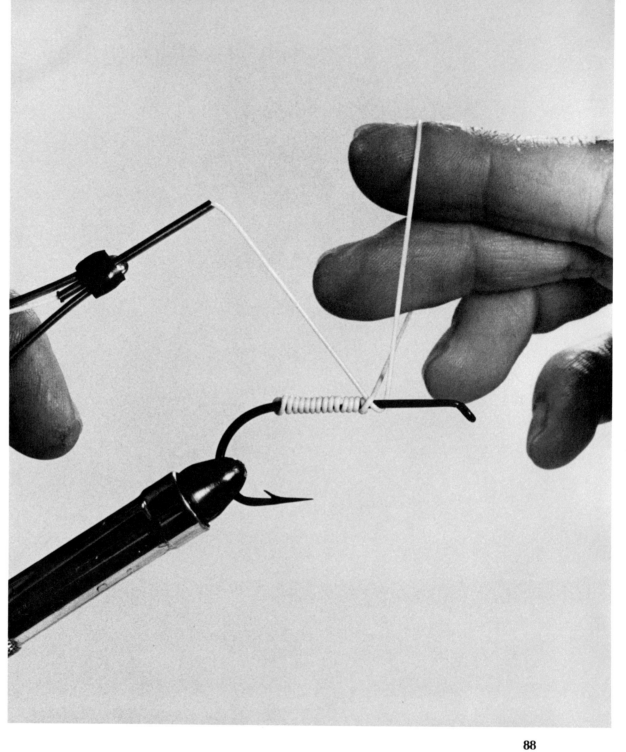

Twist your hand and hold loop to the rear, as seen in the Photo.

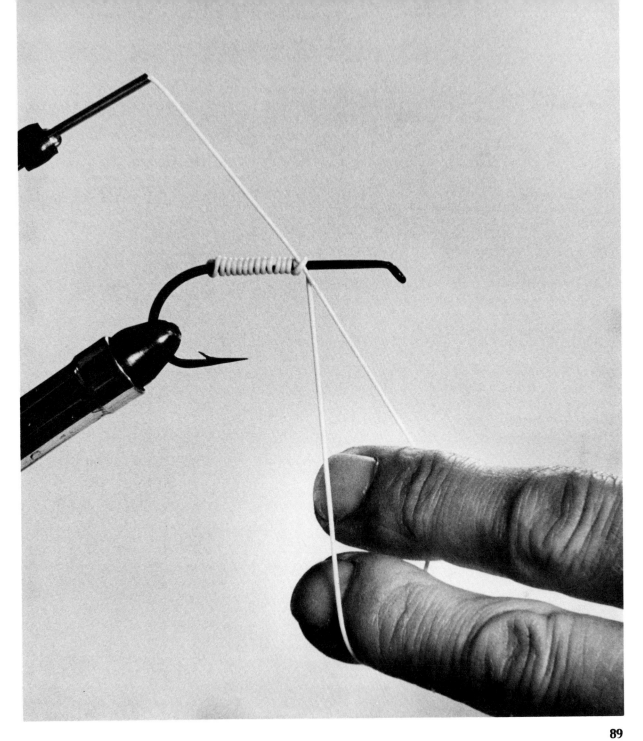

Move loop directly down.

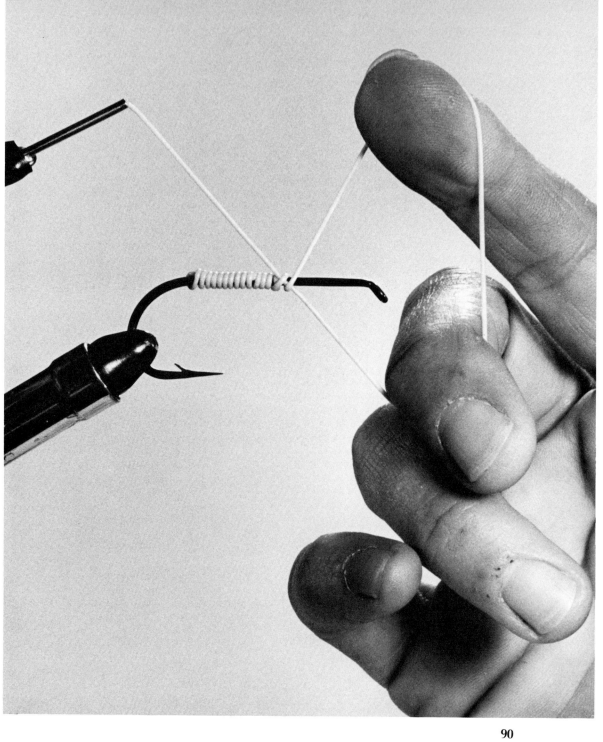

78

Open loop with your fingers on the near side and the first turn is completed.

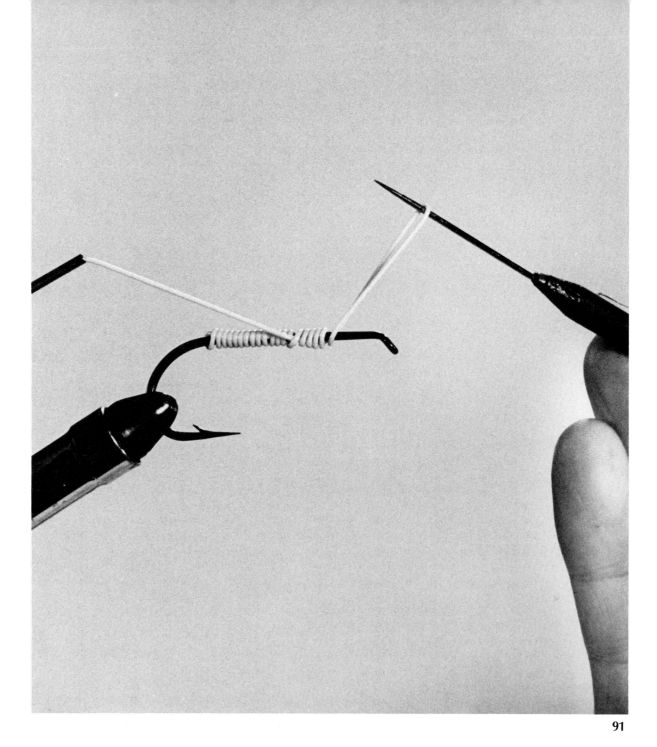

Apply several more turns in the same manner, then re-move your finger and insert the dubbing needle in the loop.

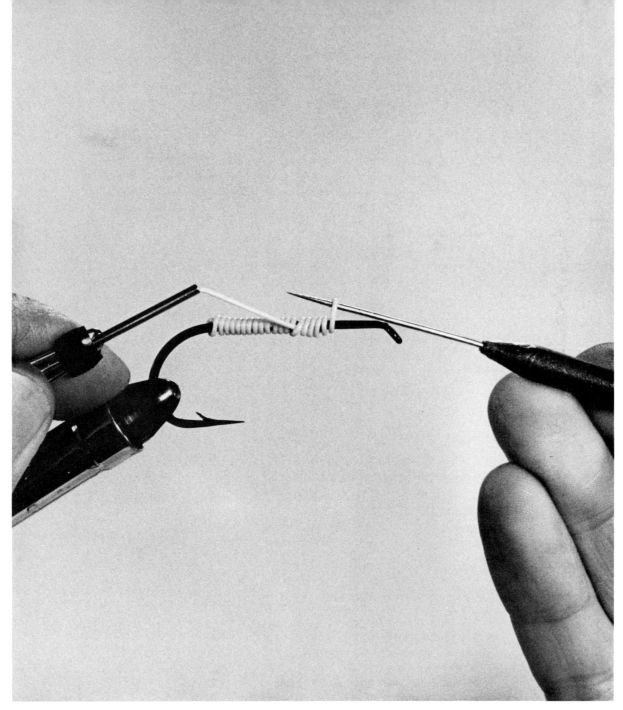

Pull the thread tight with your bobbin hand and the whip finish is completed. Cut the surplus thread and you are ready to apply head cement.

THE MANUAL HALF HITCH

Release four to six inches of Thread A between your bobbin and Windings D.

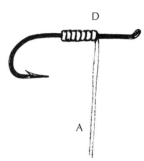

Grasp A with your fingers and form Loop B. Place the index finger and thumb of your bobbin hand at Point C, holding the thread tight between C and D.

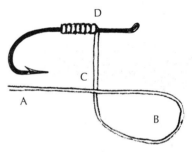

Lift Loop B up and slide it over the hook-eye onto the shank close to the windings D. Place middle finger at Point D on the far side, trapping windings and loop thread while pulling loop tight.

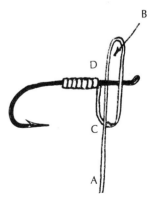

5

WET FLIES AND THEIR DRESSINGS

I have yet to meet an angler who didn't have a favorite wet-fly pattern. Studies have revealed that some mayfly species leave their nymphal stage earlier than others and the dun appears while the nymph is on its way to the surface. When this occurs, the wet fly is extremely effective and deadly. The following patterns have been selected from thousands of flies recorded by anglers and fly-tiers throughout the world. I am sure that you will find a few that will work well for your area.

Beginners should carefully read and practice the instructions given in Chapter Four, as well as familiarizing themselves with the materials mentioned in the dressings.

Regular-weight hooks may be used for wet flies, but flies tied on 1X or 2X Stout hooks will sink faster and deeper. Use heavy hooks if deep fishing is called for.

Standard Wet Flies

ALDER

Hook   Sizes 10 to 14, Regular or 2X Long
Tail   None
Body   Peacock herl
Wing   Dark mottled brown turkey-quill sections
Hackle   Black hen or coch-y-bondhu
Head   Black

BLACK GNAT

Hook   Sizes 8 to 16, Regular or 2X Long
Tail   None
Body   Black chenille
Wing   Gray goose or duck-quill sections
Hackle   Black hen
Head   Black

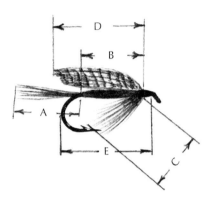

WET FLY PROPORTIONS
(For Regular Length Hook)

A = B
B = Body Length
C = From base of D to hook point
D = E
E = Hook Length

BLUE DUN

Hook	Sizes 10 to 16, Regular or 2X Long
Tail	Soft blue-dun hackle fibers
Body	Muskrat fur dubbing
Wing	Blue-gray duck-quill sections
Hackle	Blue-dun hen
Head	Black

COACHMAN

Hook	Sizes 12 and 14, Regular or 2X Long
Tail	None
Tag	Flat gold tinsel
Body	Peacock herl
Wing	White duck quill
Hackle.	Reddish-brown hen
Head	Black

Note: The Leadwing Coachman is the same as the Coachman except that it is tied with a dark-gray wing.

GOLD-RIBBED HARE'S EAR

Hook	Sizes 8 to 14, Regular or 2X Long
Tail	Soft brown hackle fibers
Body	Hare's ear fur dubbing, ribbed with flat gold tinsel
Wing	Light gray duck quill sections
Hackle	Fur picked-out in front
Head	Black

GREENWELL'S GLORY

Hook	Sizes 10 to 14, Regular or 2X Long
Tail	None
Tag	Flat gold tinsel
Body	Green floss ribbed with flat gold tinsel
Wing	Dark gray goose or duck-quill section
Hackle	Dark-brown furnace
Head	Black

GRIZZLY KING

Hook	Sizes 10 to 14, Regular or 2X Long
Tail	Narrow goose-quill section dyed red
Body	Green floss ribbed with flat gold tinsel
Wing	Gray mallard flank feather
Hackle	Cream badger
Head	Black

HENDRICKSON, DARK

Hook	Sizes 12 to 16, Regular or 2X Long
Tail	Wood-duck flank feather fibers
Body	Grayish brown fur dubbing
Wing	Wood-duck flank feather
Hackle	Blue-dun hen
Head	Black

LIGHT CAHILL

Hook	Sizes 12 to 18, Regular or 2X Long
Tail	Wood-duck flank feather fibers
Body	Cream fox-fur dubbing
Wing	Wood-duck flank feather
Hackle	Light ginger
Head	Cream tying thread

MARCH BROWN (American)

Hook	Sizes 10 to 14, Regular or 2X Long
Tail	Brown hackle fibers
Body	Brown fur dubbing ribbed with flat gold tinsel
Wing	Dark mottled turkey-quill sections
Hackle	Brown and grizzly hen, mixed
Head	Black

McGINTY

Hook	Sizes 8 to 12, Regular or 2X Long
Tail	Dyed red-hackle fibers with short teal flank-feather section over
Body	Alternate bands of yellow and black chenille
Wing	White-tipped turkey tail, white-tipped squirrel tail, or white-tipped blue mallard secondary wing-quill sections, or no wing
Hackle	Reddish-brown hen
Head	Black

MONTANA NYMPH

Hook	Sizes 8, 4X Long
Tail	A few strands of short black crow feather
Abdomen	Black chenille
Thorax	Yellow chenille ribbed with dyed black soft hackle
Wing Pad	Two strands of black chenille tied over thorax and hackle
Head	Black

MONTREAL

Hook	Sizes 8 to 12, Regular or 2X Long
Tail	Dyed red-hackle fibers
Body	Claret floss ribbed with flat gold tinsel
Wing	Brown mottled turkey-quill sections
Hackle	Dyed claret hen
Head	Black

NONDESCRIPT

Hook	Size 18, 1X Long, with 15 turns of .010" lead wire
Tail	Four or five mallard flank-feather fibers
Body	Beaver-fur dubbing dyed buff
Head	Cream

OLIVE QUILL

Hook	Sizes 10 to 14, Regular or 2X Long
Tail	Dyed olive hackle fibers
Body	Peacock quill, stripped and dyed olive
Wing	Dark-gray wing-quill section
Hackle	Hen, dyed olive
Head	Black

ORANGE COLE

(See Photo in Chapter Four)

Hook	Sizes 8 to 14, Regular or Short Shank
Tail	Golden-pheasant crest
Body	Yellow floss ribbed with gold tinsel
Wing	White-tipped squirrel
Hackle	Orange, wound after wing is attached

ORANGE FISH HAWK

Hook	Sizes 8 to 14, Regular or 2X Long
Tail	None
Body	Orange wool yarn ribbed with gold tinsel
Wing	None
Hackle	Soft badger
Head	Black

PARMACHENE BELLE

Hook	Sizes 10 to 12, Regular or 2X Long
Tail	Red and white hackle fibers
Tag	Flat gold tinsel
Body	Yellow wool ribbed with flat gold tinsel
Wing	White duck quill with narrow dyed red duck quill section on the side, in middle of wing
Hackle	One dyed red and one white, wound together mixed
Head	Black

PICKET PIN

Hook	Sizes 8 to 12, 2X Long
Tail	Brown hackle fibers
Body	Peacock herl palmered with brown hackle
Wing	White-tipped squirrel tail
Hackle	None
Head	Peacock herl segment wound in front of wing

PROFESSOR

Hook	Sizes 10 to 12, Regular or 2X Long
Tail	Dyed red-hackle fibers
Body	Yellow floss ribbed with flat gold tinsel
Wing	Gray mallard flank feather
Hackle	Dark ginger hen
Head	Black

QUILL GORDON

Hook	Sizes 12 to 16, Regular or 2X Long
Tail	Blue-dun hackle fibers
Body	Stripped peacock quill
Wing	Wood-duck flank feather
Hackle	Blue-dun hen
Head	Black

RIO GRANDE KING

Hook	Sizes 8 to 12, Regular or 2X Long
Tail	Dyed yellow hackle fibers
Tag	Flat gold tinsel
Body	Black chenille
Wing	White-duck quill sections
Hackle	Brown hen
Head	Black

SIXTEEN OR BETTER

(Originator: George Rogers)

Hook	Size 16 Regular, weighted with 20 turns of .010″ lead wire
Tail	Four or five strands from cock-pheasant tail feather
Abdomen	Beaver fur dubbing dyed buff color, ribbed with fine copper wire
Thorax	Buff beaver fur dubbing
Wing Case	Crow wing-quill section
Legs	Natural Mallard flank-feather fibers
Head	Cream

George Rogers, of Aberdeen, Maryland, who is among the finest nymph anglers in the East, also uses a smaller nymph called the Nondescript, which is not shown in the color plate. This nymph is very effective when fished upstream shortly before a *Caenis* hatch.

TELLICO NYMPH

Hook	Sizes 10 to 14, Regular or 2X Long
Tail	Brown hackle fibers
Body	Heavy yellow floss, ribbed with peacock herl
Wing Pad	Three strands of peacock herl tied over back of nymph full length
Hackle	Brown hen wound as a collar
Head	Black

WICKHAM'S FANCY

Hook	Sizes 10 to 12, Regular or 2X Long
Tail	Brown hackle fibers
Body	Flat gold tinsel palmered with brown hackle
Wing	Gray-duck quill sections
Hackle	Brown hen
Head	Black

YELLOW SALLY

Hook	Sizes 10 to 16, Regular or 2X Long
Tail	Dyed yellow quill section
Tag	Flat gold tinsel
Body	Yellow floss ribbed with flat gold tinsel
Wing	Dyed yellow duck-quill section
Hackle	Dyed yellow hen
Head	Black

6

DRY FLIES AND THEIR DRESSINGS

The tying methods explained in Chapter Four will enable you to tie all the following patterns. I've found all these patterns effective at one time or another.

Midge flies are very popular among dry-fly purists, and there are times when they are deadly, even for large brown and rainbow trout. A number of the most popular ones are included in the list of dressings. My friend Tony Ottomano insists that certain well-known patterns, such as the Adams, Blue Quill, Blue Dun, and Black Gnat, tied on size 20 or 22 hooks will take more fish more often than any other flies.

Standard Dry Flies

ADAMS

Hook	Sizes 10 to 22
Tail	Grizzly and brown hackle fibers, mixed
Body	Muskrat-fur dubbing
Wing	Grizzly hackle tips
Hackle	Grizzly and brown, wound mixed
Head	Black

BADGER BIVISIBLE

Hook	Sizes 10 to 16
Tail	Badger hackle fibers
Body	None
Wing	None
Hackle	Badger tied palmer with white hackle wound in front next to hook eye *Note:* Bivisible patterns are tied in many colors, e.g., brown, blue dun, ginger, black, and grizzly. All have a white hackle wound in front.

BLUE DUN

Hook   Sizes 10 to 22
Tail   Blue-gray hackle fibers
Body   Muskrat-fur dubbing
Wing   Blue-gray mallard wing-quill sections
Hackle   Blue-gray
Head   Black

BROWN OLIVE

Hook   Sizes 10 to 16
Tail   Brown hackle fibers dyed olive
Body   Dark-olive silk floss coated with clear cement
Wing   Blue-gray hackle tips
Hackle   Brown, dyed olive
Head   Black

CAENIS

(Originator: John M. Snider)

Hook   Sizes 24, up-eyed
Tail   Three stiff grizzly-hackle fibers
Body   Black, 7/0 prewaxed tying thread (Male) or White, 6/0 silk thread (Female)
Hackle   Grizzly

FOX

Hook   Sizes 12 to 20
Tail   Honey-colored hackle fibers
Body   Muskrat-fur dubbing
Wing   Gray mallard wing-quill sections
Hackle   Honey
Head   Black

GRIZZLY WULFF

Hook   Sizes 8 to 12
Tail   White bucktail
Body   Pale yellow floss, fur dubbing, or wool
Wing   White bucktail, divided
Hackle   Grizzly and brown, mixed
Head   Black

GRAY FOX VARIANT

(Originator: Preston Jennings)

Hook   Sizes 10 to 14, short shank
Tail   Ginger hackle fibers
Body   Flat gold tinsel
Wing   None
Hackle   Ginger with grizzly mixed
Head   Black

Note: Other variant patterns are dressed with blue-dun or cream hackle, both with gold-tinsel bodies and tied on short-shanked hooks. These over-size hackle flies were created to imitate the larger species of mayflies. The hackle should be two or three times the normal length for a given size hook with a rather long tail.

GRAY WULFF

(Originator: Lee Wulff)

Hook   Sizes 8 to 12
Tail   Brown bucktail
Body   Gray wool yarn
Wing   Brown bucktail, divided
Hackle   Blue-gray
Head   Black

Note: Two other fine Wulff patterns, not shown in the color plates, are just as effective as the Gray Wulff

HENDRICKSON
(Originator: Roy Steenrod)

Hook	Sizes 12 to 16
Tail	Medium blue-dun hackle fibers
Body	Pinkish fur dubbing (vixen of red fox)
Wing	Wood-duck flank feather
Hackle	Medium blue dun
Head	Yellow tying thread with reddish-brown tinting cement

LIGHT CAHILL

Hook	Sizes 12 to 22
Tail	Very light ginger hackle fibers
Body	Cream fur dubbing
Wing	Wood-duck flank feather
Hackle	Very light ginger
Head	Cream

MARCH BROWN

Hook	Sizes 10 to 16
Tail	Ginger hackle fibers
Body	Light fawn-colored fur from red fox
Wing	Wood-duck flank feather
Hackle	Dark ginger and dark grizzly, mixed
Head	Yellow tying thread with orange tinting cement

QUILL GORDON

Hook	Sizes 12 to 22
Tail	Rusty blue-dun hackle fibers
Body	Stripped two-toned peacock quill
Wing	Wood-duck flank feather
Hackle	Rusty blue dun
Head	Pale yellow

RED QUILL
(Originator: Preston Jennings)

Hook	Sizes 12 to 22
Tail	Medium blue dun
Body	Dark-brown hackle stem, stripped
Wing	Wood-duck flank feather
Hackle	Medium blue dun
Head	Yellow tying thread with reddish-brown tinting cement

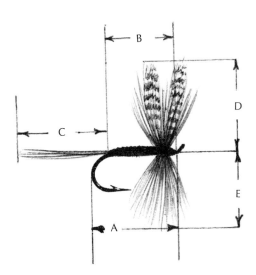

DRY FLY PROPORTIONS
(For Regular Length Hook)

A = Hook Length
B = Front of A to above Barb Point
C = A
D = A
E = 1-1/2 to 2 times the Hook Gap

ROYAL WULFF
(Originator: Lee Wulff)

Hook	Sizes 8 to 14
Tail	White calf tail
Body	Two peacock-herl butts, one at the tail, one in back of the wing, separated by center band of red floss
Wing	White calf tail, divided
Hackle	Dark brown
Head	Black

WHITE WULFF

Hook	Sizes 8 to 12
Tail	White bucktail
Body	Cream fur dubbing or wool
Wing	White bucktail, divided
Hackle	Cream badger
Head	Black

89

SPIRIT OF PITTSFORD MILLS
(Originator: Stephen P. Belcher)

Hook	Sizes 12 to 16
Tail	Ginger hackle fibers
Body	Grayish-white duck down, dubbed and ribbed with clipped ginger hackle
Wing	Light-grizzly hackle tips
Hackle	Light ginger
Head	Pale-yellow tying thread

SULPHUR DUN
(Originator: Vince Marinaro)

Hook	Size 16
Tail	Pale blue dun
Body	Sulphury yellow fur dubbing
Wing	Pale blue-dun hackle tips
Hackle	Pale blue dun
Head	Pale yellow tying thread

Midge Patterns

BADGER MIDGE

Hook	Sizes 20 to 28
Tail	None
Body	Peacock quill, stripped
Wing	None
Hackle	Badger

BLACK GNAT

Hook	Sizes 20 to 28
Tail	Black hackle fibers
Body	Peacock quill, stripped
Wing	Black quill sections (crow or dyed duck quill)
Hackle	Black

BROWN MIDGE

Hook	Sizes 20 to 28
Tail	Brown hackle fibers
Body	One strand cock-pheasant tail fiber
Wing	None
Hackle	Brown

CREAM MIDGE

Hook	Sizes 20 to 28
Tail	Cream hackle fibers
Body	Cream fur
Wing	None
Hackle	Cream

DUN MIDGE

Hook	Sizes 20 to 28
Tail	Dark blue-dun hackle fibers
Body	Dun grey fur.
Wing	None
Hackle	Dark blue dun

GREEN MIDGE

Hook	Sizes 20 to 28
Tail	Pale-olive hackle fibers
Body	Olive hackle stem, stripped
Wing	None
Hackle	Light olive

93

Blue Dun
Size 20

Black Gnat
Size 20

Caenis
Size 24

Adams
Size 20

7

FUR NYMPHS

Many anglers fail to realize the importance of nymphs when selecting their fly patterns; yet, experts estimate that fish do approximately eighty-five per cent of their feeding below the surface, which leaves the dry-fly purist with only fifteen per cent of the action.

My friend Wayne I. Leonard of Harrisburg, Pennsylvania, is one of the finest nymph fishermen in the East. He has researched and developed a series of nymphs, which he has generously let me present in this chapter. Wayne insists that fur from seal, beaver, otter, mink, muskrat, and many other fur-bearing animals is far superior to any other material for nymph dressings.

Before attempting to tie the fur nymphs, you must learn the important step of making a "fur chenille," using the spinning method described in Chapter Four under the heading "Fur Bodies." Some patterns may require fur of several shades that must be mixed. This is done by a special method explained in Chapter Three.

94

THE MARCH BROWN NYMPH
(Stenonema vicarium)

Length	10 to 16 mm
Hook	Mustad #3906-B, size 12 or 14
Thread	Pale yellow, prewaxed 6/0
Tail	Three fibers from wood-duck flank feather, same length as body
Abdomen	Tannish-gray fur, flat and tapered
Thorax	Medium-brown mink fur
Wing Case	Same as thorax

Start the nymph by attaching your tying thread in the usual manner and tie in the tail. Form a 3" spinning loop in the end and wind the thread forward to one-third of the hook length from the eye (on a 4X Long hook, to one quarter of the hook length). Cut a thin layer of light tannish-gray fur from the edge of a piece of skin with your scissors. (See Photo **95**.) Place it in the loop close to the hook and spread it to a thin 1½″ long layer with the fibers crossways. Spin a fur chenille and wind it on the hook to the thread position, brushing back the fur for each turn. Tie it off and cut away the surplus. Now trim the fur with your scissors on all sides to form a flat, tapered abdomen as shown in Drawing **96**.

To make the thorax and wing case, form another spinning loop directly in front of the abdomen. While the fiber length of the fur used for the abdomen is of little consequence, the thorax fur should not be less than ½″ long, so that you can form the wing case when it is trimmed. Select a piece of mink fur and prepare a fur chenille as before. Wind it forward to the eye and tie it off. Cut off the surplus and wind a small head before applying a whip-finish knot or some half-hitches. Now trim the thorax even with the abdomen on the bottom and two sides. Tease up the fur on the top and trim the rear part of the thorax even with the rest. A thin portion is

left long in front for the wing case, as seen in Drawing **97**. Trim the wing-case fur to one third of the total nymph length and round-off the corners a little. Press it back flat over the thorax with your fingers and a little moisture. At times I brush the wing case fur into shape of the nymph wing with head cement. A small brush from a nail polish bottle works nicely. This represents the undeveloped wings, replacing the conventional quill section. The finished nymph is shown in Photo **94**. (Also see Photo **98**.)

All the nymph patterns (and the Shrimp and the Cress Bug) are tied using this method. Perhaps you have some favorites of your own that are not included in my list but which can easily be converted and tied like the Fur Nymphs. Since these nymphs are not weighted, they can be fished at any depth, including directly on the surface. For bottom fishing or in fast streams, it may be necessary to wrap a little strip lead on your leader to get them where the fish are feeding.

95

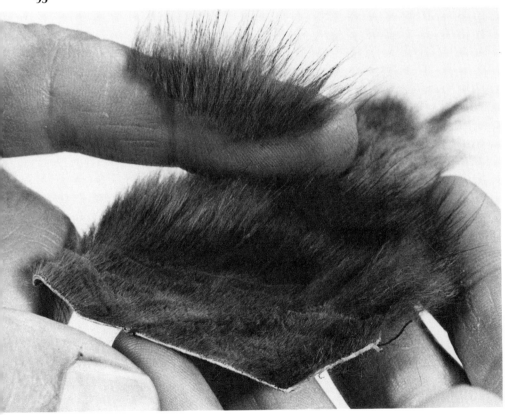

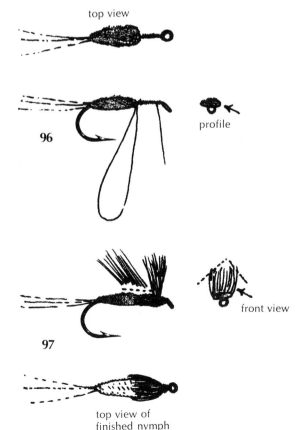

top view

96

profile

97

front view

top view of
finished nymph

Fur Nymph Patterns
(Developed by Wayne I. Leonard and the author)

BLUE-WINGED DUN
(Paraleptophlebia adoptiva)

Length	7 to 9 mm
Hook	#3908, sizes 16 and 18
Thread	Black, prewaxed 6/0
Tail	Three wood-duck fibers
Abdomen	Dark reddish-brown mink
Thorax	Very dark-gray beaver
Wing Case	Same as thorax

BLUE-WINGED OLIVE
(Baetis vagans)

Length	6 to 8 mm
Hook	#3906, sizes 16 and 18
Thread	Black, prewaxed 6/0
Tail	Three wood-duck fibers
Abdomen	Olive seal fur
Thorax	Blackish-brown beaver fur
Wing Case	Same as thorax

BROWN DRAKE
(Hexagenia atrocaudata)

Length	25 mm
Hook	#79580, size 8, 4X Long
Thread	Black, prewaxed 6/0
Tail	Three very narrow gray ostrich herls
Abdomen	Medium-brown mink fur
Thorax	Very dark reddish-brown mink fur with guard hairs left in
Wing Case	Same as thorax

CAENIS
(Tricorythodes atratus)

Length	3.5 mm
Hook	#3906, size 20
Thread	Olive, prewaxed
Tail	Three wood-duck fibers
Abdomen	Medium otter fur
Thorax	Medium-brown mink fur
Wing Case	Same as thorax

GREEN DRAKE
(Ephemera guttulata)

Length	20 to 25 mm
Hook	#79580, size 8, 4X Long
Thread	Black, prewaxed 6/0
Tail	Three, rusty ostrich herl tips, length of hook gap
Abdomen	Rusty mink over amber rabbit fur
Thorax	Rusty mink
Wing Case	Same as thorax

HENDRICKSON
(Ephemerella subvaria, rotunda, and invaria)

Length	9 to 12 mm
Hook	#3906-B, sizes 12 and 14
Thread	Black, prewaxed 6/0
Tail	Three wood-duck fibers
Abdomen	Medium-brown mink
Thorax	Reddish-brown mink (dark)
Wing Case	Same as thorax

MICHIGAN MAYFLY NYMPH
(Hexagenia limbata)

Length	20 to 30 mm
Hook	#79580, sizes 8 and 10, 4X Long
Thread	Black, prewaxed 6/0
Tail	Three ginger hackle tips trimmed bushy, same length as hook gap
Abdomen	Creamy tan over medium-brown mink
Thorax	Dark brown fur
Wing Case	Same as thorax

Brown Drake

March Brown
Caenis
Blue Wing Olive

98

QUILL GORDON
(Iron fraudator and *Epeorus pleuralis)*

Length	Approximately 10 mm
Hook	#3906-B, sizes 12 and 14
Thread	Gray, prewaxed 6/0
Tail	Two wood-duck fibers
Abdomen	Gray fur over medium-brown mink
Thorax	Very dark gray or black fur
Wing Case	Same as thorax

SULPHUR
(Ephemerella dorothea)

Length	6 to 9 mm
Hook	#3906-B, sizes 16 and 18
Thread	Gray, prewaxed 6/0
Tail	Three wood-duck fibers
Abdomen	Pale-cream seal fur
Thorax	Tannish-gray otter with guard hairs
Wing	Same as thorax

WHITE FLY
(Ephoron leukon)

Length	12 to 14 mm
Hook	#79580, size 16, 4X Long
Thread	Gray, prewaxed
Tail	Three wood-duck fibers
Abdomen	Gray-white seal fur
Thorax	Medium or dark-gray otter fur
Wing Case	Same as thorax

WESTERN GREEN DRAKE
(Ephemerella grandis)

Use Brown Drake Nymph

WHITE-GLOVED HOWDY
(Isonychia bicolor)

Length	12 to 16 mm
Hook	#36680, size 12, 3X long
Thread	Gray, prewaxed 6/0
Tail	Three rusty-amber ostrich herls, length of hook gap
Abdomen	Reddish-brown mink fur
Thorax	Same as abdomen
Wing Case	Same as abdomen; tinted with black felt pen

SHRIMP
(Gamarrus)

Hook	#3906-B, size 16
Thread	Olive, prewaxed 6/0
Body	Same as Cress Bug, but clipped top and sides only

CRESS BUG
(Isopodo)

Hook	#3906-B, size 16
Thread	Olive, prewaxed
Body	Muskrat, dyed olive, over medium-brown mink, clipped top and bottom

95

8
EMERGED DUNS

"This is wild," I yelled to Tom Cooney, who was fishing fifty feet below me. "I've never seen anything like it." I was referring to an evening hatch of the White Fly *(Epheron leukon)*, which comes off like clockwork on the Yellow Breeches in Allenberry, Pennsylvania during August and September. The hatch was so heavy that it looked like a snowfall. I reached out and grabbed a few flies with my bare hands and put them in my collecting jar. Looking like tiny sailboats, the newly hatched duns floated for a short distance with their wings upright before taking off for the trees. The fish went wild. Thirty minutes later, when the hatch was over, Tom asked me how many fish I had landed. It was then that I suddenly realized I had completely forgotten to fish.

Similar hatches of other mayflies of importance to the angler occur on streams in other parts of the country throughout the trout season.

The flies best suited for this type of fast fishing and short floats are the emerged duns, which are dressed with fur body, an upright wing, and a stiff tail that is spread out a little. The fly has no hackle but floats beautifully, aided by the roughly trimmed fur, flat bottom, and guard hair around the wing and thorax. It helps to add a little line grease. Incidentally, a little line grease can also be smeared on the wing to keep it upright and compact.

THE WHITE FLY
(Epheron leukon)

Hook	Mustad #94842, size 14, up-eye
Thread	White, prewaxed 6/0
Tail	Three, light otter guard hairs
Body	White seal fur, spun and trim tapered, leaving it rough on sides and in front to aid floating
Wing	White fur bunch with guard hair, tied upright

Start by tying in the tail so it spreads out a little like a fan, and take the thread to a third of the hook length from the eye. Cut a small bunch of white fur and tie it in as an upright wing, using the tying method explained in Chapter Four. Trim and taper the butt ends of the wing. The fly should now appear as shown in Drawing **100**. Bind the fur ends down on the hook shank as you wind the tying thread to the tail. Form a 4″ spinning loop. Insert some white seal fur in the loop and follow the illustrated instructions in Chapter Four. Make a 2″-long fur chenille and wind it on the hook past the wing and tie off close behind the eye. Cut off the surplus and apply a drop of cement on the windings. The fly should now look as in Drawing **101**. Now trim the rear portion of the body, rounding and tapering it. The bottom and top in front of the wing can also be trimmed and tapered down close to the eye, but the sides in front are trimmed just a little, so the bushy side fur will aid the fly in floating and help keep it upright on the surface. Study the finished fly shown in Photograph **99** for the correct trimming (also see Photo **102**).

Some patterns may require fur of several shades, which must be mixed. This is done by the method explained in Chapter Three.

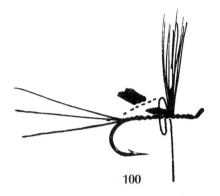

100

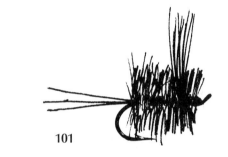

101

102

White Fly   March Brown

Caenis

Western Green Drake

Emerged Dun Patterns

(Developed by Wayne I. Leonard and the author)

BLUE-WINGED DUN

(*Paraleptophlebia adoptiva*)

Hook   #94842, sizes 16 and 18
Thread   Black, prewaxed 6/0
Tail   Three stiff brown otter guard hairs spread well apart
Body   Pale-olive seal fur over reddish-brown mink
Wing   Muskrat fur bunch with guard hair

BLUE-WINGED OLIVE

(*Baetis vagans*)

Hook   #94842, sizes 14 to 22
Thread   Olive prewaxed 6/0
Tail   Two otter guard hairs, spread apart
Body   Olive seal fur over medium-brown mink
Wing   Medium-gray fur bunch with guard hair

BROWN DRAKE

(*Ephemera simulans*)

Hook   #94842, size 10
Thread   Yellow prewaxed 6/0
Tail   Three ginger hackle fibers, spread apart
Body   Pale-yellow rabbit over medium-gray mink fur
Wing   Fur bunch, gray and brown mixed, with guard hair left in

GRAY FOX

(*Stenonema fuscum*)

Same as March Brown but tied on a size-14 hook

GREEN DRAKE

(*Ephemera guttulata*)

Hook   #94831, size 8, 2X Long
Thread   Yellow prewaxed 6/0
Tail   Three stiff light moose-mane hairs, flared
Body   Light tan over pale-yellow seal fur
Wing   Fur bunch, gray and olive mixed, with guard hair left in

HENDRICKSON (Female)

Same as the male but dressed with a body of cream fur over a very small amount of pale-pink rabbit fur

HENDRICKSON (Male)

(*Ephemerella subvaria, rotunda,* and *invaria*)

Hook   #94842, sizes 12 and 14
Thread   Black prewaxed 6/0
Tail   Three otter guard hairs, spread apart
Body   Medium-brown mink fur
Wing   Blue-gray fur with guard hair

LIGHT CAHILL

(*Stenonema canadense* and *ithaca*)

Hook   #94842, size 14
Thread   Yellow prewaxed 6/0
Tail   Two light-ginger hackle fibers, spread apart
Body   Light-cream fur
Wing   Tan fur bunch with guard hairs

MARCH BROWN
(Stenonema vicarium)

Hook	#94842, sizes 10 and 12
Thread	Primrose prewaxed 6/0
Tail	Two stiff brown guard hairs, spread apart
Body	Creamish-tan fur over small amount of amber seal
Wing	Tan fur bunch with guard hair, slanted back

WHITE GLOVED HOWDY
(Isonychia bicolor)

Hook	#94842, sizes 10 and 12
Thread	Black prewaxed 6/0
Tail	Two ginger hackle fibers, spread apart
Body	Reddish-brown mink or seal fur
Wing	Dark gray fur bunch with guard hair

MICHIGAN MAYFLY
(Hexegenia limbata)

Hook	#94831, size 8, 2X Long
Thread	Yellow prewaxed 6/0
Tail	Four to six light elk hairs, divided and tied in a wide V shape
Body	Pale-yellow seal over tan fur
Wing	Gray muskrat bunch mixed with olive rabbit, with guard hair left in

QUILL GORDON
(Iron fraudator and Epeorus pleuralis)

Hook	#94842, sizes 12 and 14
Thread	Gray, prewaxed 6/0
Tail	Two otter guard hairs, spread well apart
Body	Pale-yellow seal fur over medium-brown mink
Wing	Gray fur bunch with guard hair

SULPHUR
(Ephemerella dorothea)

Hook	#94842, sizes 16 to 18
Thread	Yellow prewaxed 6/0
Tail	Three stiff light-ginger hackle fibers, spread apart
Body	Pale-yellow fur over pale-orange fur
Wing	Light blue-gray fur with guard hair

WESTERN GREEN DRAKE
(Ephemerella grandis)

Hook	#94831, size 10, 2X Long
Thread	Green prewaxed 6/0
Tail	Three stiff olive hackle fibers, spread apart
Body	Green seal or rabbit fur
Wing	Dark blue-gray fur bunch with guard hair

WHITE FLY
(Ephoron leukon)

See page 96

9

CUT-WING PARACHUTE DUNS

(Tying method and patterns
originated by the author)

I doubt that any other type of dry fly has a more realistic and graceful float than a well-tied parachute dun. They should certainly not be overlooked by anglers needing flies for long floats and fast-water fishing.

The tying procedure is practically the same as for a regular dry fly, and with the exception of the following techniques, all necessary instructions, including the preparation of cut wings, can be found in Chapter Four. The first deviation from conventional dry-fly construction occurs when the tail has been tied in. Instead of being left parallel with the hook shank, the tail is raised upward to a forty-five-degree angle. This is best accomplished by taking two or three turns of thread directly around the fibers close to where they leave the hook. Then raise the tail to the prescribed angle with your fingers and apply a little tension on the thread before taking two or three turns around the hookshank to hold the tail up at an angle. Add a drop of cement on the windings and take your tying thread to the wing position, a third of the hook length from the eye.

The cut wings are attached in the same manner as hackle-tip wings. After being secured on the hookshank, they are raised to an upright position and held there by several turns of thread around the hook shank and the stems at the base of the wings. Since the hackle is to be later wound directly around the wing base, it is important to leave a little bare stem between the lower fibers of the wing and the hook shank. Apply some cement on the wing windings. Your fly should now be as illustrated in Drawing **103.**

Roll some fur on the tying thread and form the rear portion of the body, from the tail to directly behind the wing. Let the tying thread hang at this position and prepare a single dry-fly hackle with an average fiber length equal to two and a half times the hook gap. Before tying in the hackle, however, take a long narrow strip of goose- or turkey-wing quill section, 1/16" to 1/8" wide, (this quill section can be omitted if you wish) and tie it in directly behind the wing on top of the hook.

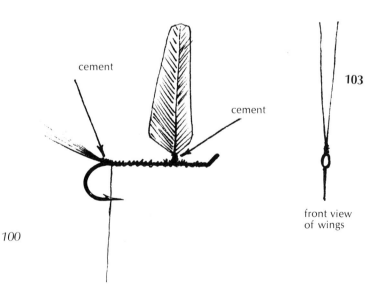

cement

cement

103

front view
of wings

The longest portion should project to the rear much like a wet-fly wing. This piece of material represents a form of wing divider and hackle retainer. It is finished off after the hackle is wound on. Now tie in the prepared hackle on top of the quill section and secure it firmly with thread windings behind and in front of the wing. Cut off the surplus materials and roll a little fur on the thread and fill in the gap close behind and in front of the wing. Wind the hackle horizontally around the wingbase, taking three or four turns without tightening it too much, then tie it off in front. (See Parachute Hackle in Chapter Four.) Cut off the surplus and clamp your hackle pliers onto the end of the quill section, which has been kept underneath the shank and out of the way while the hackle was wound on. Take it up through the hackle fibers and carry it forward between the two wings. Take it down through the fibers in front and tie it down on the shank with a couple of turns of thread. Now carefully pull it tight, which will set the wings upright and divided. Secure the strip firmly with more thread windings, then cut off the surplus material and wind the head.

To make the fly more durable, add some clear cement on the head and on the quill strip between the wings. I sometimes add a drop of cement on the outside of the base of the wings with my dubbing needle, pressing down any flared-up hackle fibers in the process.

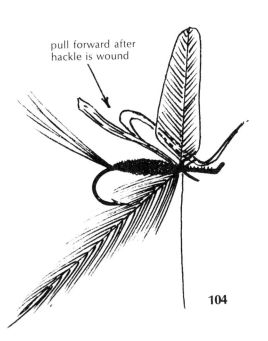

pull forward after hackle is wound

Green Drake
Cutwing Parachute Dun

Patamanthus

Little Blue May Fly

Hendrickson Male

Parachute Patterns

The following flies are all dressed with wings that are cut to shape. Use Mustad No. 94842 up-eyed Hooks. I believe these patterns can be fished successfully almost anywhere, but by all means collect some specimens of some of your local mayflies as models for new patterns. By using the preceding tying instructions, you can easily supplement the pattern list to suit your particular needs.

BLUE WING OLIVE

Hook	Sizes 16 and 18
Thread	Olive prewaxed size 6/0
Tail	Medium blue-dun hackle fibers
Body	Yellowish-olive fur and very small amount of medium brown fur, mixed
Wing	Dark blue-gray
Hackle	Cream badger

EPHORON

Hook	Size 14
Thread	White prewaxed size 6/0
Tail	Pale blue dun hackle fibers
Body	White fur
Wing	White
Hackle	Creamish white

FRAUDATOR

Hook   Size 14
Thread   Gray prewaxed size 6/0
Tail   Rusty blue dun hackle fibers
Body   Pale yellow and medium brown fur, mixed
Wing   Dark blue-gray
Hackle   Rusty blue dun

GREEN DRAKE

Hook   Size 10
Thread   Yellow prewaxed size 6/0
Tail   Light elk-mane hair
Body   Cream fur mixed with very light yellow and light olive furs
Wing   Wood-duck flank feather or mallard
Hackle   Cream badger dyed pale chartreuse

HENDRICKSON (Male)

Hook   Size 14
Thread   Black prewaxed size 6/0
Tail   Medium blue dun hackle fibers
Body   Reddish-brown fur
Wing   Dark blue-gray
Hackle   Medium blue dun

HENDRICKSON (Female)

Same as above, but dressed with a body of cream fur mixed with a small amount of pink fur, or vixen from red fox.

ISONYCHIA

Hook   Size 12
Thread   Yellow prewaxed size 6/0, tinted brown
Tail   Ginger hackle fibers
Body   Reddish-brown fur, fairly dark
Wing   Dark blue-gray
Hackle   Dark ginger

LIGHT CAHILL

Hook   Size 14
Thread   Yellow prewaxed size 6/0
Tail   Pale ginger hackle fibers
Body   Light cream fur
Wing   Ginger
Hackle   Pale ginger

LITTLE BLUE MAYFLY

Hook   Sizes 18 and 20
Thread   Gray prewaxed size 6/0
Tail   Light blue dun hackle fibers
Body   Pale olive and reddish-brown fur, mixed
Wing   Dark blue-gray
Hackle   Medium blue dun

MARCH BROWN

Hook   Sizes 12 and 14
Thread   Yellow prewaxed size 6/0, tinted primrose
Tail   Ginger hackle fibers
Body   Creamish-tan fur
Wing   Ginger
Hackle   Dark ginger

POTAMANTHUS

Hook   Size 12
Thread   Yellow prewaxed size 6/0
Tail   Pale yellow hackle fibers
Body   Creamish yellow fur
Wing   Creamish yellow
Hackle   Pale yellow or light honey

SULPHUR

Hook   Size 16
Thread   Yellow prewaxed size 6/0
Tail   Light ginger hackle fibers
Body   Sulphur-yellow fur
Wing   Very light blue dun
Hackle   Very light ginger

10

FUR SPINNERS

To become a spinner, the mayfly must complete its second transformation, or molt. Mating and egg laying take place shortly after the molting, and the life cycle of the mayfly has ended. The spinners fall in the water with their wings spread out, and artificials created to imitate them are known to the angler as spent-wing patterns. Good spinner imitations are rare, which is usually owing to poor construction and bad judgment in the material selected by commercial fly-tiers.

The prominent English angler J. C. Mottram in his book *Fly Fishing: Some New Arts and Mysteries*, published in 1913, briefly describes the Silhouette Olive Duns, calling them "flies of the future." One of these patterns relies not on hackle but on its fur body to keep it afloat.

The spinners dealt with here are constructed in a manner similar to Mottram's no-hackle fly but with some valuable modifications made in the tail and wing dressing. These changes make the flies extremely effective and durable—and they float well.

HENDRICKSON FUR SPINNER (Male)
(Ephemerella subvaria, rotunda, and invaria)

Hook	#94842, size 14
Thread	Black prewaxed 6/0
Tail	Four to six stiff blue-dun hackle fibers, divided and tied in an open V shape
Body	Reddish-brown mink or seal fur
Wing	Light blue-dun hackle wound and fashioned half- or full-spent

Place the hook in your vise and attach the tying thread. Select some good stiff hackle fibers and tie them in as a tail in the usual manner. The next step is of considerable importance, so take your time doing it correctly. Divide the tail fibers into two equal groups and bring your tying thread up between the groups. Make some crisscross windings to fix the two groups of fibers in a wide V

shape, and apply a drop of clear cement to hold them securely. The tails should extend at the same level as the hook shank, or slightly below it, so as to act as outriggers to stabilize the fly in the surface film. The tail should appear as illustrated in Drawing **108**.

The spinner body is now dressed in the same manner as those for Fur Nymphs and Emerged Duns. Form a spinning loop in the tail end and take the tying thread forward to one third of the hook length from the eye. Now insert the fur in the loop and spin a 2″ fur chenille, which is wound on the hook and tied off at the thread position. (If body fur is to be mixed, see instructions in Chapter Three.) Cut off the surplus fur chenille and take a couple of extra windings over the end. As before, the fur must be brushed back with your fingers for each winding when forming the body. Each winding should be laid as close to the other as possible. This forms the rear portion of the body, which can now be trimmed rough, so that the long fur will not interfere as the wings are tied in.

Select a light-blue-dun hackle of the best dry-fly quality and measure the length of the fibers located in the middle of it. To qualify for a wing, these fibers should be equal to the length of the hook. Prepare the hackle in the same manner as an ordinary dry-fly hackle (explained in Chapter Four) and attach it in front of the body as shown in Drawing **109**. Wind it on the hook with five or six close turns, and tie it off. Cut off the surplus and work the fibers into two wings by gathering them in equal-sized bunches and crisscrossing the tying thread. If a few fibers escape and are not bunched, cut them away with your scissors. The wings should be fixed in a half-spent position, that is, both slanting up a little from the horizontal, one on each side, as shown in Drawing **110** at nearly right angles to the hook. Push the wing construction back close to the body, but leave room for one more turn of fur between them. Apply a drop of cement to the wing base and windings. Take the tying thread behind the

wing and form another spinning loop and fur chenille. Wind the first turn of fur behind the wing and the remainder in front. Push the windings back a little, compressing the fur in front of the wing. Tie off close to the eye and whip-finish. Now trim the fur body to shape, taking particular care around the tail and wings; they should not be trimmed. The finished fly is shown in Photo **107**.

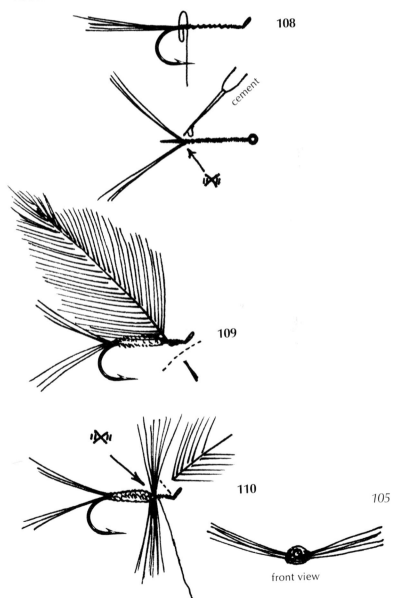

108

cement

109

110

front view

Fur Spinner Patterns

(Standard patterns modified into fur spinners by the author)

BLUE-WINGED DUN
(Paraleptophlebia adoptiva)

Hook	#94842, sizes 16 and 18
Thread	Black prewaxed 6/0
Tail	Four to six medium dark blue dun hackle fibers divided and tied in an open V shape
Body	Reddish-brown mink fur
Wing	Dark blue-dun hackle wound and fashioned half-spent

BLUE-WINGED OLIVE
(Baetis vagans)

Hook	#94842, sizes 14 to 22
Thread	Olive prewaxed 6/0
Tail	Four to six otter guard hairs divided and tied in an open V shape
Body	Olive seal fur over medium-brown mink
Wing	Light blue-dun or grizzly hackle wound on and fashioned half-spent

GRAY FOX
(Stenonema fuscum)

Same as March Brown but tied on a size-14 hook

GREEN DRAKE (Coffin Fly)
(Ephemera guttulata)

Hook	#94831, size 8, 2X Long
Thread	White prewaxed 6/0
Tail	Four moose mane hairs, divided and tied open in a V shape
Body	White seal fur, 1/8" at tail end tinted dark gray with marking pen
Wing	Dark grizzly wound on and fashioned half-spent

HENDRICKSON (Male)
(Ephemerella subvaria, rotunda, and *invaria)*

See page **104**

HENDRICKSON (Female)

Hook	#94842, sizes 12 and 14
Thread	Yellow prewaxed 6/0
Tail	Four to six stiff blue-dun hackle fibers divided and tied in a V shape
Body	Cream fur over pale-yellow seal fur
Wing	Light blue-dun hackle wound on and fashioned half- or full-spent

LIGHT CAHILL

(Stenonema canadense and ithaca)

Hook	#94842, size 14
Thread	Cream prewaxed 6/0
Tail	Four to six light-ginger hackle fibers, divided and tied open in a V shape
Body	Cream fur
Wing	Grizzly hackle wound on and fashioned spent

MARCH BROWN

(Stenonema vicarium)

Hook	#94842, sizes 10 and 12
Thread	Primrose prewaxed 6/0
Tail	Four to six stiff ginger hackle fibers, divided and tied open in a V shape
Body	Creamish-tan fur
Wing	Grizzly hackle wound on and fashioned half-spent

MICHIGAN MAY FLY

(Hexagenia limbata)

Hook	#94831, size 8, 2X Long
Thread	Yellow prewaxed 6/0
Tail	Four to six elk mane hairs, divided and tied in an open V shape
Body	Pale-yellow seal fur
Wing	Grizzly hackle wound on and fashioned half-spent

QUILL GORDON

(Iron fraudator and Epeorus pleuralis)

Hook	#94842, sizes 12 and 14
Thread	Gray prewaxed 6/0
Tail	Four to six light-blue-dun hackle fibers divided and tied in an open V shape
Body	Pale-yellow seal fur over medium-brown mink
Wing	Light blue-dun hackle wound and fashioned spent-wing

SULPHUR

(Ephemerella dorothea)

Hook	#94842, sizes 16 and 18
Thread	Yellow prewaxed 6/0
Tail	Four to six stiff blue-dun hackle fibers, divided and tied open in a V shape
Body	Cream seal fur over pale-yellow rabbit fur
Wing	Light blue-dun hackle wound on and fashioned half-spent

WESTERN GREEN DRAKE

(Ephemerella grandis)

Hook	#94831, size 10
Thread	Black prewaxed 6/0
Tail	Four to six brown hackle fibers, divided and tied in an open V shape
Body	Reddish-brown mink
Wing	Blue-dun hackle wound on and fashioned half-spent

WHITE FLY

(Ephoron leukon)

Hook	#94842, size 14
Thread	White prewaxed 6/0
Tail	Four or six light-blue-dun hackle fibers divided and tied open in a V shape
Body	White seal or rabbit fur
Wing	White hackle wound on and fashioned half-spent

11

STONE FLIES
AND
CADDIS FLIES

Bill Blades used to carry a box full of large stone-fly nymphs in his fishing vest and frequently caught more fish with them than other fly fishers struggling with long, fine leaders and small dry flies. Almost anywhere you fish, the nymphal skins of large stone-fly creepers can be seen lying on rocks or floating down the stream. Very early in the season, before any of the important mayflies arrive, a much smaller member of the stone-fly family appears. These are known to anglers and fly-tiers as the Little Brown Stone Fly. Although there are hundreds of members in the stone-fly family, the creeper and the little brown stone fly have long been accepted as the only two of real importance to the fisherman. I usually carry a small aquarium dip net and some collecting jars with me to the stream, so I can collect some specimens and study the color and size of the flies in the area where I am fishing.

STONE FLY CREEPER

Hook	Size 8, 4X Long (sometimes weighted with lead wire for fast sinking)
Thread	Yellow prewaxed 6/0
Tail	Two body-length brown hackle stems, stripped
Feelers	Two half body-length brown hackle stems, stripped
Abdomen	Tan gift-wrapping yarn, cemented, flattened, and ribbed with brown floss
Thorax	Same as abdomen but without ribbing
Legs	Cock-pheasant tail fibers or stripped hackle stem half body length
Wing Case	Two sections of brown mottled turkey wing quill, notched in one end to form V shapes
Tinting	Brown marking pen, on windings on top of thorax only

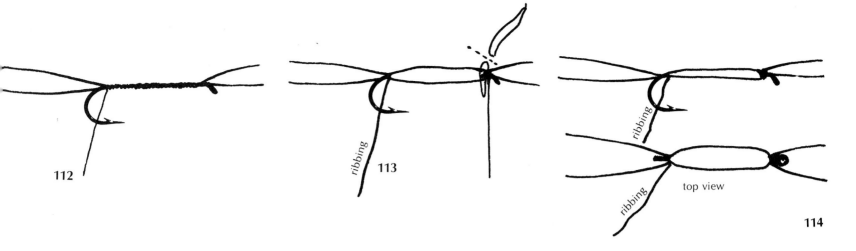

112

113

ribbing

114

ribbing

top view

ribbing

Strip the fibers from four brown rooster neck hackles and tie them in as shown in Drawing 112. Attach a 6" length of brown floss at the tail position for ribbing, and wind your tying thread forward to 1/8" from the eye. Take a single strand of yarn and split it in the middle lengthwise. Roll one of the pieces with your fingers a little to make it fairly firm. Tie it in at the thread position and wind it on the shank to form a body 1/8" in diameter, tapered down at the tail. Wrap from the thread position down to the tail end and then back again. Tie off the yarn directly behind the eye and trim away the excess material. Form a very small head on the shank over the end of the yarn before applying half hitches or a whip finish, then cut the thread. The fly should now appear as in Drawing 113.Saturate the entire yarn body with clear head cement and flatten it with pliers when it has dried a little. See Drawing 114

Attach your tying thread in the middle of the body, then wind the ribbing on the rear half of the body (abdomen) and tie in the first pair of legs, which are made from a single strand of pheasant tail tied in on the far side and then taken across the top of the body and tied down on the near side with several turns of thread, as shown in Drawing 115.Make a half hitch and bring the thread forward on top to a position one third the length of the front body half (thorax) and tie in the second pair of legs.

The wing cases are now prepared from 7/16" wide quill sections,coated with rubber or vinyl cement and dried, as shown in Drawing 116 . Tie in first wing case at the same position as the second pair of legs, raising it up a little by drawing the tying thread tight. Take the tying thread to where the third pair of legs will go and add a couple of turns of thread to bind down the surplus end from the first wing case. After you've trimmed away the excess material, your fly should appear as in Drawing 117. Now tie in the third pair of legs and the second wing case. Take several extra turns of thread, then apply half hitches or a whip finish. Trim the second wing-case end close behind the eye, as shown in Drawing 118.

The windings used when attaching the wing cases are now tinted with a brown marking pen, after which the entire nymph is given several coats of clear cement. Trim the legs to size and your Stone Fly is finished (see Photograph 111).

115   side view

116

117

top view

118

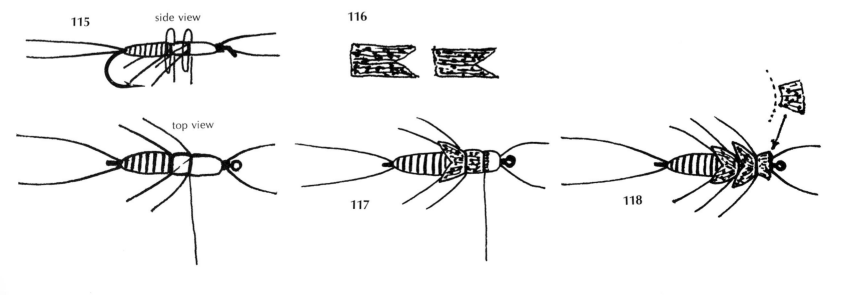

119

LITTLE BROWN STONE FLY
(Tacniopterix fasciata)

Hook	Sizes 14 and 16, 2X Long
Silk	Yellow
Body	Six to eight 1/2" long gray-brown tail fibers from cock pheasant
Tail	Two cock-pheasant fibers, a half the length of the body
Legs	Cock-pheasant tail fibers, three on each side
Feelers	Two cock-pheasant tail fibers
Wings	Two dark-blue-dun hackle tips tied flat the length of the body
Head	1/16" long—formed with tying thread and lacquered with chestnut-colored head cement

120

To tie this fly, begin by wrapping the hook shank with tying thread from the eye to a point above the barb. Select six to eight of the longest cock-pheasant tail fibers you have and tie them in with the tips extending about half the body length beyond the bend. Secure them firmly and hold up the long ends while winding the tying thread toward the front, as shown in Drawing **120**.

Form the body by winding all the long ends on the hook shank at the same time, making sure the first turn covers the tie-in windings. Tie them off behind the eye and cut off the surplus with your scissors, then trim off the tips at the back of the body, leaving two for the tails. Continue winding the tying thread down the body to 1/8″ from the eye, as in Drawing **121**.

Take three cock-pheasant tail fibers and lay them on top of the body with the tips on the far side. Slanting the tips toward the back and down a little and secure them with two or three turns of thread. Now tie in three more tail fibers, on the near side, slanting them to match the three on the other side. The length of the legs should be approximately half that of the body. Secure them firmly with extra turns of thread and a little clear head cement. Cut off a fiber end from each side for the antennae or feelers, and tie them in. Trim all the legs to a uniform length. (See Drawing **122**.)

Tie in two blue-dun hackle tips on top. They should be the same length as the body and laid flat. Take four or five extra turns of thread to form the head. Whip finish and apply chestnut-colored head cement. The finished Stone Fly is shown in Photo **119**.

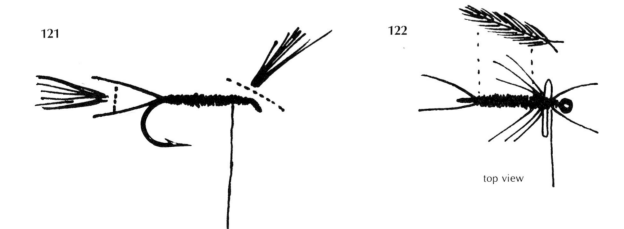

121

122

top view

Caddis Flies

CINNAMON CADDIS (Wet)

Hook	Size 12, 2X Long
Thread	Yellow prewaxed 6/0
Tail	None
Body	Tan fur dubbing
Wing	Cinnamon turkey-tail quill sections cut to shape and tied down-wing
Legs	Ginger hen hackle
Horns	Dark moose mane
Head	Yellow thread tinted with light brown tinting cement

Make the fur body by using the twist dubbing method and apply the hackle in front of the body, as explained in Chapter Four (see Drawing **123**).

Cut a 1/2" wide section from a cinnamon turkey-tail quill and double it lengthwise before trimming it to shape.(See Drawing **124**.) Tie in the wing in a down-wing position, as shown in Drawing **125.** You will notice that this type of down wing is tied in by the tip end of the quill section, so as to form a low rooflike wing over the body. Trimming takes place in the heavy end. To prevent splitting, coat the quill sections with rubber or vinyl cement. This can be done either before or after the wing is tied in. Secure the wing tightly and cut off the excess material.

The two horns (feelers) are now tied in, as shown in Drawing **125.** Cut off the surplus and wind the tapered head before tying off with half hitches or a whip finish. Apply some tinting cement on the windings. Your finished Caddis Fly should look like Photo **126.**

123

quill section

124

trim

wing

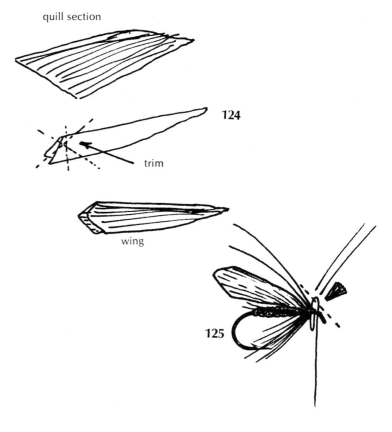

125

CINNAMON CADDIS (Dry)

This fly is tied in the same manner as the wet version, except that a dry-fly hackle and hook are used. The hackle consists of a short-fibered ginger hackle palmered over the body. The wing is then tied in and the front hackle wound in dry-fly style. To help keep the fly in an upright position on the water, I sometimes trim the lower portion of the hackle to a V shape. I do this on the palmered hackle as well as on the front floating hackle. Use the same tying method for the two additional patterns given below.

DARK BLUE SEDGE (Dry)

(Not the original dressing)

Hook	Sizes 12 or 14
Thread	Gray prewaxed 6/0
Tail	None
Body	Brown fur dubbing palmered with dark blue-dun hackle
Wing	Gray mallard or goose quill sections, cut to shape and tied down-wing
Hackle	Dark blue dun
Horns	Moose mane
Head	Gray

Note: The wet version is tied on a heavier hook, without the palmered hackle and with a soft hen hackle used instead of the floating hackle.

LITTLE BLACK CADDIS

Hook	Size 16
Thread	Black
Body	Muskrat fur dubbing palmered with black hackle
Wing	Black crow-wing quill section, cut to shape and tied down-wing
Hackle	Black
Horns	Moose mane
Head	Black

For the following imitations of the caddis larva and pupa, follow the relevant tying instructions given in Chapter Four.

CADDIS CASE

Hook	Size 10, 2X Long
Body	Hare's ear or squirrel fur dubbed with the spinning method and trimmed rough
Legs	Sparse partridge hackle, wound as a collar
Head	Black

CADDIS WORM

Hook	Sizes 8 to 12, 2X Long
Body	Rear two thirds, white fur ribbed with white tying thread; front third, brown seal fur
Hackle	Sparse brown partridge, wound as a collar
Head	Black

GREEN CADDIS

Hook	Sizes 8 to 12, 2X Long
Body	Rear two thirds, light-olive seal fur ribbed with white tying thread; front third, grayish-brown fur dubbing
Legs	Sparse brown partridge, wound as a collar

Caddis Case

Green Caddis

116

128

12

THE DARBEE CRANE FLY

Although crane flies are not considered to be of any great importance, there are times when trout, smallmouth bass, and panfish feed on them. Rainy days will generally bring crane flies out of hiding, and since their flight is rather clumsy, they often crash land on the water surface. Making a good imitation of these delicate, long-legged insects has long been a problem. Most anglers use spiders and variants to imitate the natural. These imitations are merely short-shanked dry-fly hooks dressed with long tails, tinsel bodies, and sparse oversize hackles. Unfortunately, spiders and variants lack the silhouette of the naturals.

Harry Darbee, the famous American angler and fly-tier from Roscoe, New York, decided there was a need for a more realistic imitation and went to work at his vise, trying various materials and manipulations. In the mid 1950s the Darbee Crane Fly was born. This fine imitation requires only two feathers for its construction.

The original Darbee Crane Fly, which is shown in Photos **128** and **129,** has a hackle and wingspan of approximately two inches. The parachute-type hackle makes it extremely well suited for skittering the fly over the surface, a form of fishing that often brings the big ones to the net.

DARBEE CRANE FLY

Hook	Sizes 8 and 10, 4X Short, up-eyed
Thread	Yellow prewaxed 6/0
Body and Wing	Mallard side feather or grand Nashua feather

Attach your tying thread on the hook shank in the usual manner and wind it to a position 1/8″ from the eye. Select a large mallard side or grand Nashua feather with fibers of the same length on both sides. The fibers should

be approximately 1½" long in the middle portion. Hold the feather by the tip and stroke the fibers down toward the base, as shown in Photo **130.** (The tip should not be cut away [as it is in the photo] until the fly is finished.) Cut the stem to 1" in length, measuring from the base of the tip. The 1" stem, with long fibers on each side and the tip still attached, is now ready to be tied in. Moisten your fingers and stroke the fibers in the direction opposite to the way they naturally bend, crowding them down along the stem as much as possible. Hold the stem and fibers very firmly between your thumb and first finger while placing them on top of the hook, with the outside of the feather up, the tip projecting forward over the eye, and the long fibers slanting back along the hook shank. Take a couple of turns of thread to secure the feather on top of the hook, as shown in Drawing **131.** Hold the fibers in place on top of the hook while drawing the stem further out over the eye until it is free of the windings and 1/16" beyond them. Take some extra turns of thread around the fibers and the hook to secure the fibers firmly. Now divide the long fibers into two parts and pull them out at right angles to the shank, taking a couple of crisscrossing X turns to hold them in spent-wing position. Grasp the body portion by the tip and fold it back between the wings to a horizontal position over the hook shank and take five or six turns of thread around the body and shank very close behind the wing. Pull the body portion up a little while pressing with your fingers in the center between the wings, to insure a very firm joint in the middle. Take a couple of half hitches, apply some clear cement on the windings and joint, and cut the thread.

130

Your fly should now appear as illustrated in Drawing **132.**

The next step is to prepare a large stiff medium blue-dun hackle with fibers as long as one of the wings. Stiff hackles of that size are not easy to get in natural blue dun. A good dyed hackle can be used instead. Since only a few turns of hackle are needed, prepare the tip portion in dry-fly fashion and tie it in by the stem in front of the wing. The hackle should sit on the hook shank with the underside up and the fibers crossways, as shown in Drawing **133.** The hackle is now wound in parachute style around the fly on the top of the hook shank. The hackle should go in tight between the body and the hook shank in the rear and ahead of the body joint on top of the hook in front. Apply two to four turns of hackle, then tie off the hackle remainder in front of the wing in the usual manner. (See also Parachute Hackle in Chapter Four.) Cut off the surplus hackle and finish off with half hitches or a whip finish. Apply some clear cement on the windings and hackle stem underneath and in front on top.

Now coat the body portion with rubber or vinyl cement and mold it into shape. Trim away the tip portion and your fly is finished. It should look like Photos **128** and **129.**

Hold the finished fly upside down high over your head and let go of it. It will not only flip over but will also make the slowest, most delicate descent you ever saw.

Many smaller species of crane flies can be tied with the Darbee method by selecting the material accordingly. The yellow and the orange flies have a wingspan of about 1″ and are tied on Size 16, 4X Short hooks and using light ginger hackle and mallard body feather, tinted on the body with marking pen.

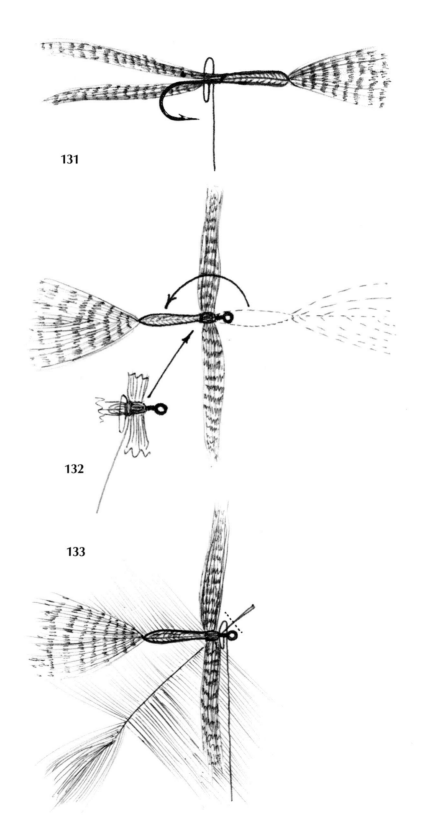

131

132

133

13
TWO-FEATHER MAYFLIES

Those spooky fish grow big up here in the Catskills," said Harry Darbee with a grin when he pulled out a small box from behind some old letters lying on his tying bench, "but I think I've found the answer to their capture." When he poured the contents of the box into my hand I knew he was right. Harry explained that only two feathers were needed to tie these delicate extension-body mayflies on 4X Short hooks: one feather for tails, body, and wing; and a second feather for the floating hackle. Harry designed these flies for fishing the long, slow stretches on the Catskill streams. They work well on placid trout water everywhere.

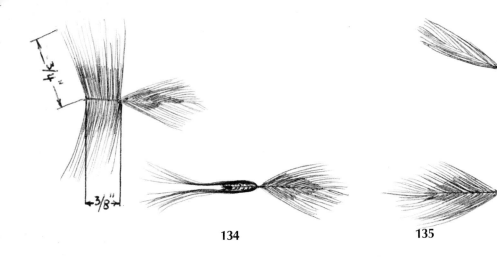

134

top view

135

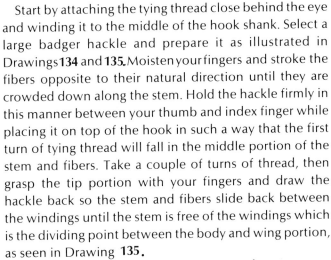

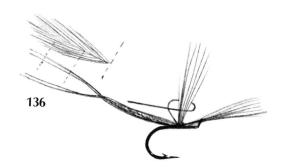

136

THE BADGER MAYFLY

Hook	Sizes 14 to 18, 4X Short, up-eyed
Thread	6/0, prewaxed
Tail, Body and Wing	Cream badger hackle
Hackle	Medium blue dun

Start by attaching the tying thread close behind the eye and winding it to the middle of the hook shank. Select a large badger hackle and prepare it as illustrated in Drawings **134** and **135.** Moisten your fingers and stroke the fibers opposite to their natural direction until they are crowded down along the stem. Hold the hackle firmly in this manner between your thumb and index finger while placing it on top of the hook in such a way that the first turn of tying thread will fall in the middle portion of the stem and fibers. Take a couple of turns of thread, then grasp the tip portion with your fingers and draw the hackle back so the stem and fibers slide back between the windings until the stem is free of the windings which is the dividing point between the body and wing portion, as seen in Drawing **135.**

Next divide the wing fibers—the long fibers pointing over the hook eye—into two equal portions, raise them to an upright and divided position, and secure them one at a time like a hair wing. (See Drawing **136** and Hair Wings Chapter Four.) Now apply a generous amount of rubber or vinyl cement on the body portion and mold it into shape. The tip portion can now be cut away, leaving four fibers (two outside fibers on each side) at the end of the

body. Put some cement on the fibers and stroke them between your fingers, so that two are joined together on each side, thus forming the two tails. To finish the fly, apply the floating hackle in the usual dry-fly fashion and tie off.

The measurements indicated in Drawing **134** will produce a fly that is close to a size-12 standard dry fly. For smaller or larger flies, these measurements can be altered accordingly. I tie these mayflies with feathers of various colors when matching a particular hatch. Many of the body feathers mentioned in Chapter Three are excellent for this purpose. The patterns that can be dressed with the Darbee two-feather method are almost endless.

An interesting variation can be obtained by tying a small bunch of wood-duck fibers on the hook at the wing position before proceeding with the regular construction procedure. The fibers should be the same length as the hackle wing portion. The surplus ends should be trimmed off close to the windings. The fibers are then raised to form a wood-duck wing, together with the hackle fibers.

121

14

IMPORTANT TERRESTRIALS (Land Insects)

The small creatures hopping in and out of your picnic basket and generally being a nuisance to your comfort during the warm summer days are also providing a considerable portion of the fish's diet. Important terrestrials of interest to the angler and fly-tier are grasshoppers, crickets, ants, leaf hoppers, beetles, and inchworms. Most of them are easy to tie. I suggest that you collect some specimens from the area you intend to fish, to determine the correct size and color for your artificials.

LETORT GRASSHOPPER
(Originator: Ed Shenk)

Hook	Sizes 10, 12, and 14, 1X Long, up-eyed
Thread	Yellow
Body	Mixed yellow, tan, and olive rabbit fur
Underwing	Brown mottled turkey wing-quill section tied flat over length of body with natural deer hair slightly longer than the wing-quill tied over the quill section and slightly flared
Wing	Deer hair (1/8" long) from wing butts

Start by mixing the fur, either as described in the dressing or to get the shade of the specimen you have collected. Form a 3" long piece of fur dubbing at the bend of the hook by using the twist dubbing method described in Chapter Four. Wind the dubbing on the shank with close turns and tie it off 1/8" from the eye. Cut off the surplus dubbing and your fly should appear as shown in Drawing **137.**

Next, cut a 5/16" wide section from a turkey wing quill and fold it double lengthwise. Cut the end to a right angle with the fibers and round the corners a little with your scissors. Tie it in on top of the hook so it lays flat along the body, reaching to the end of it. Trim off the surplus feather in front and let the thread hang at the

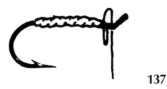

137

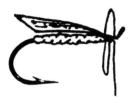

138

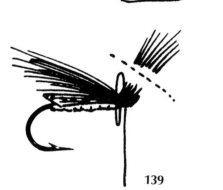

139

tie-in position as shown in Drawing **138.** Before proceeding I sometimes brush some liquid rubber or vinyl cement on the wing to prevent it from splitting, but the turkey feather is usually pretty solid.

To make the over-wing cut a small bunch of natural deer hair from the hide, leaving it full length. Remove the fuzz and shorter hairs and even up the tips as much as possible. Hold the hair firmly between your fingers and tie it in with five or six turns of tying thread. Pull the thread tight to bind the hair securely on the shank. This will also make the hair flare out as it should. Now hold back the butt ends with your fingers while taking several turns of thread in front of them before tying-off with a whip finish or half hitches. Apply a generous amount of clear head cement on the windings, both on top and underneath. Hold the butt ends with your fingers and trim them off with your scissors, leaving them 1/8" long to form the head. (See Drawing **139**) The Hopper is finished.

Cricket

The Cricket is tied in the exact same manner as the Hopper, but it is completely black and is generally much smaller, with sizes 14 and 16 being the most popular. Black fur dubbing, dyed-black deer body hair, and a section of crow wing quill make up the dressing.

During my summer fishing I have found that the same hopper-type fly, tied on size 16 or 18 hooks in all green, all yellow, or even all white, will take fish when nothing else works.

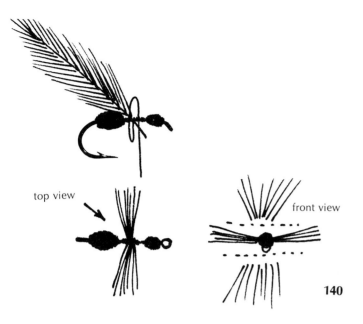

top view

front view

140

Red and Black Ants

BLACK ANT

Hook   Sizes 14 through 22, Regular length

Body   Two black fur lumps, large at the bend and smaller in front

Hackle One rusty blue dun tied in middle of the hook as spent wing, clipped top and bottom

Attach some 6/0 prewaxed black tying thread and wind it to the hook bend. Apply some black fur on the tying thread by using the roll-dubbing method explained in Chapter Four. Wind it on the shank, forming the larger of the two lumps. Peel off any excess fur or slide it down the thread. The bare thread is now wound forward to 1/16″ from the eye, where a second slightly smaller lump is formed using the same method of dubbing. Remove any excess fur from the tying thread and wind it to the middle of the hook, as shown in Drawing **140.**

Select a rusty blue-dun hackle with fibers the same length as the fly body. Remove the soft fibers at the base and tie it in at the thread position. Wind on the hackle in the same manner as a regular dry-fly hackle. Tie off the hackle and apply a drop of clear cement on the windings. The hackle is now trimmed top and bottom, leaving only the fibers on the sides to imitate a spent wing.

The tying instructions for the Red Ant are the same as for the Black Ant, but instead of black fur, a golden-brown dubbing is used for the two body lumps. The hook sizes are the same, but for some reason the Red Ant seems to produce better when tied on smaller hooks.

Ants are not very good swimmers and do not float high on the water like a conventional dry fly, but rather in the surface film or even half submerged. Wet-fly variations of the Ant call for a small change in the material. Instead of being made of fur lumps, the two body sections are formed with tying thread and enameled. Everything else is the same.

Black Deer Hair Beetle

Hook   Sizes 14 through 20 (Mustad #94833)

Body   Black or orange nymph thread wound over deer body hair

Back   Deer hair folded over body and tied down in front

Head   Trimmed deer-hair butts from back material

Legs   Deer hair trimmed to size

To tie the Deer Hair Beetle, start by attaching your orange or black nymph thread on the shank 1/8″ from the eye (for a size-14 hook). Wind it to the bend and back to the starting position. Cut a small bunch of black deer hair and even up the tips. The amount of hair needed depends on the size fly you are working on. With a little experience you will soon be able to choose a suitable bunch. Tie in the hair on top of the hook with several turns of nymph thread. The tips of the hair should project a hook length forward over the eye. These tips will be used for legs later. Bind down the deer hair on the shank by winding the nymph thread over it all the way to the bend. Make sure the hair stays on top of the hook or you will have trouble later when forming the back of the beetle. Wind the nymph thread forward again to the starting position and tie it off with a couple of half hitches. Cut the nymph thread and apply some clear cement to the body. The fly should now appear as illustrated in Drawing **141.**

Attach some black tying thread 1/8" from the eye, then divide the hair tips into two equal parts. Crisscross the tying thread between the two parts while working them into place so that a bunch projects out at a right angle from each side of the hook, much like a spent wing. With your scissors, reduce the number of fibers to three on each side, and the legs are finished, except for being cut to the correct length, which will be determined later. Your fly should now appear as shown in Drawing **142.** Take your tying thread to a position directly in front of the legs, then grasp all the hair which is projecting to the rear and fold it forward and tight over the body. Bind it down in front with several turns of thread and tie off with a whip finish or half hitches.

Trim the butt ends close behind the eye to form the head. Apply some clear cement on the windings and trim the legs to size, as shown in Drawing **143** Since deer hair applied in this fashion is easily torn by the fish's teeth, a generous amount of thin rubber or vinyl cement is applied on the back and sides of the finished Beetle.

I make the Beetle in other colors besides black, including green, yellow, blue, and natural deer hair. They all work well at various times. In fact, I fish with someone from time to time who uses nothing but Beetles for trout and panfish alike.

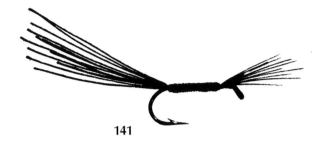

141

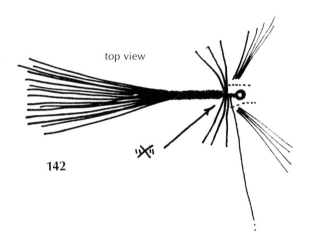

top view

142

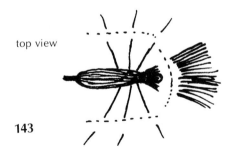

top view

143

125

Letort Hopper

Black Ant

Cricket

Leaf Hopper

Green Inch worm

Black Beetle

Red Ant

Leaf Hopper

(Originator: John M. Snider)

Hook	Mustad #94833, size 22
Thread	White 7/0 prewaxed
Body	Light-gray Caribou hair
Wing Cover	Gray or rust-colored grouse tail segments

This fly is very simple in its construction, but its small size may cause some difficulty. Frankly speaking, spinning caribou hair on size-22 hooks is not my favorite pastime, but the Leaf Hopper is one fly I would not want to be without. John Snider, who is a well-known Pennsylvania angler has seduced many large brown's in the storied limestone streams in his famous trout state on this minute leaf hopper.

Start the fly by tying in a six-fiber segment of grouse tail. This segment should be tied in on top of the hook, at the tail position, with the dull side up and should extend 3/4" beyond the bend so it can be folded over later, like the back on the Deer Hair Beetle. Spin small bunches of caribou hair on the shank in the manner explained in Chapter Sixteen (Deer Hair Flies). Allow space behind the eye so the wing cover can be tied down later. Trim the caribou hair to shape with your scissors so that is flat on the bottom and rounded on the sides and top, as shown in Drawing **145**.

Grasp two strands of grouse tail and pull them forward over the middle of the back. Tie them down in front with a turn or two of thread, then pull the rest of the fibers forward, laying two strands on each side of the center ones and slightly down on the sides. Tie them down in front, cut off the surplus material, and wind a small head before tying off with a whip finish or half hitches. Apply a little cement on the windings, and the fly is finished.

This fly is extremely effective during July and August on flat stretches of streams and on placid ponds bordering wooded areas. For maximum effectiveness, it must be fished very slowly on a 6X or 7X tippet. By all means, collect some specimens from your area and match them in size and color.

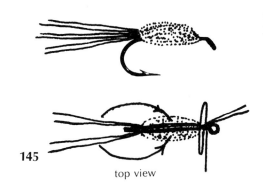

145

top view

127

GREEN INCH WORM

Hook Mustad #94833, size 12
Thread Yellow or light green prewaxed 6/0
Body Yellowish-green bucktail, segmented with tying thread and extended beyond the hook bend

The bucktail best suited for this fly is located close to the base of the tail. The hair in that location is hollow like the body hair, though much longer.

Cut a small bunch of hair close to the hide, leaving it full length. Remove all the fuzz and short hairs from the bunch and tie it in on the hook directly behind the eye with the butt ends projecting 1½" forward over the eye. Let the hair roll around the shank and tighten the windings securely before applying some clear cement. Now wind the tying thread to a position 1/8" from the eye and your fly. The fly should now appear as illustrated in Drawing 146. Now double the long butt ends back over the eye and along the hook shank and hold them tight together with the rest of the hair while taking six or eight tight turns of thread around them, thus forming the first segment, as shown in Drawing 147.

Shift the thread 1/8" toward the rear and form another segment. Continue in this manner down the shank and beyond the bend, where the rest of the body is formed as an extension. (See Drawing 148.) Including extension, the body should be ¾" to 1¼" long and approximately ⅛" in diameter. When the desired body length has been reached, tie off the thread with several half hitches and pull them tight. Cut off the surplus hair and give the entire body a good coat of clear head cement. The finished Inch Worm is shown in Photo 149.

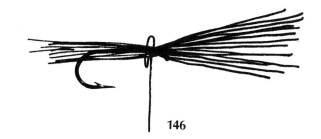

146

147

148

BALSA POPPERS

left to right

Balsa Gerbubble Bug
Red Head Badger

Black Badger Popper
Red and White B.P.

Brown and Grey B.P.
Yellow and Black B.P.

Bucktail Frog Popper
Yellow Frog Popper

Coch-y-Bondhu Popper
Redhead Skipper

Orange and Grizzly B.P.
Striper Skip-Bug

SALMON FLIES

left to right

Blue Charm
Hairy Mary
Professor

Darbee Spate Fly
Jock Scott
Silver Grey

Garry
Jungle Hornet
Rusty Rat

Green Highlander
Lady Joan
Sweep

Grizzly King
Logie
Hunt's Wasp (dry)

Colonel Monel (dry)
Rat-Faced McDougal (dry)
Pink Lady Palmer (dry)

STEELHEAD FLIES

left to right

Alaska Mary Ann
Fall Favorite
Skykomish Sunrise

Badger Hackle Peacock
Golden Demon
Skunk

Brad's Brat
Kennedy Special
Thor

Burlap
Orleans Barber
Wind River Witch

Comet
Purple Peril
Western Steelhead Bee

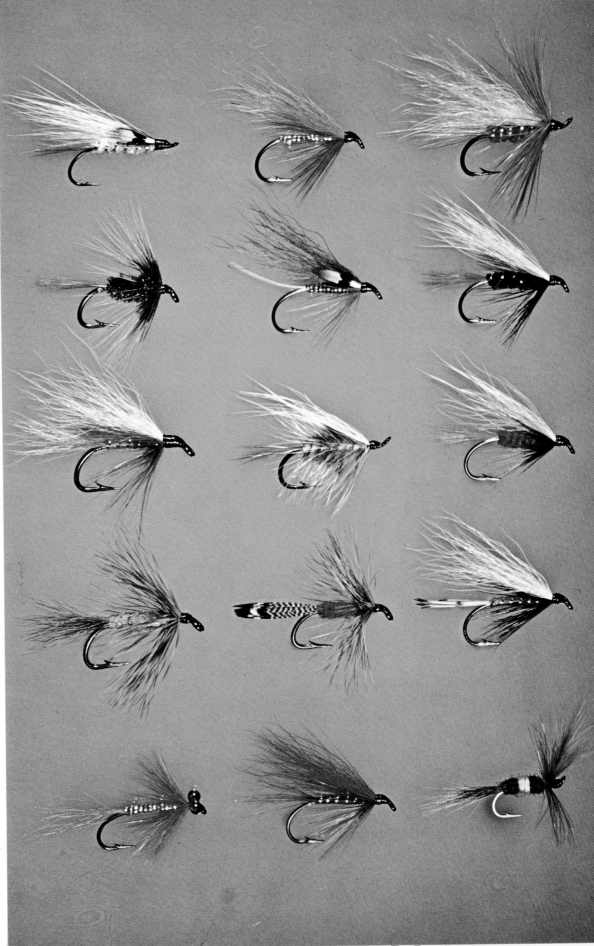

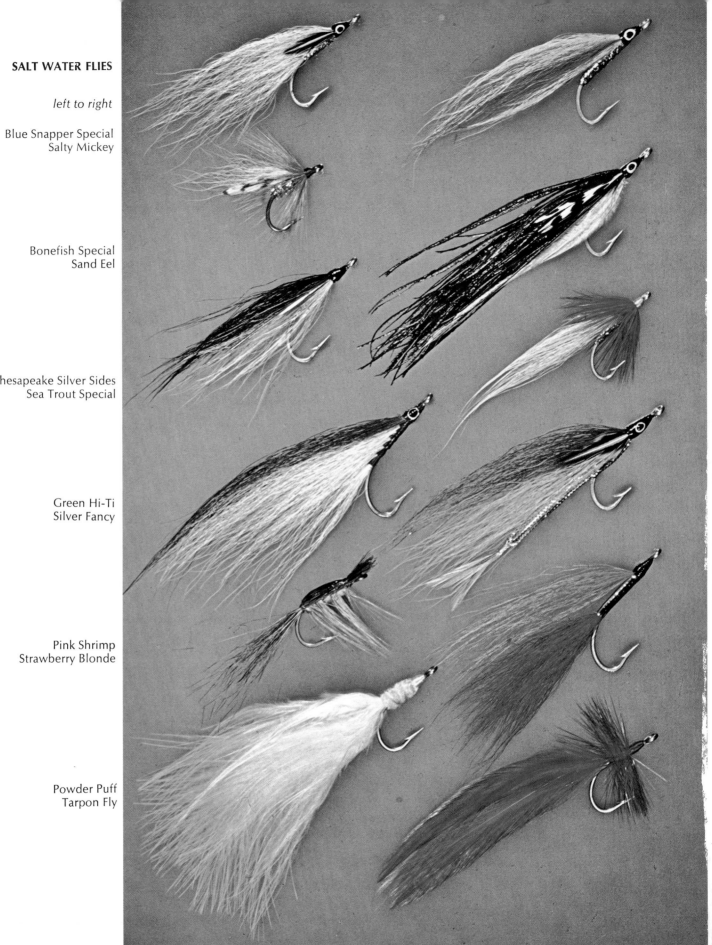

SALT WATER FLIES

left to right

Blue Snapper Special
Salty Mickey

Bonefish Special
Sand Eel

Chesapeake Silver Sides
Sea Trout Special

Green Hi-Ti
Silver Fancy

Pink Shrimp
Strawberry Blonde

Powder Puff
Tarpon Fly

Woolly Worms

I use size-8 salmon hooks for most of my Woolly Worms. They are all tied with a short red-wool butt and grizzly hackle palmered over a chenille body, and finished with a red head. To avoid using red enamel on the head, I use thin red nylon nymph thread for the entire fly. The series consists of six flies that differ only in the colors of their chenille bodies, which are black, red, yellow, orange, green, and brown.

15
BUCKTAILS
AND STREAMERS

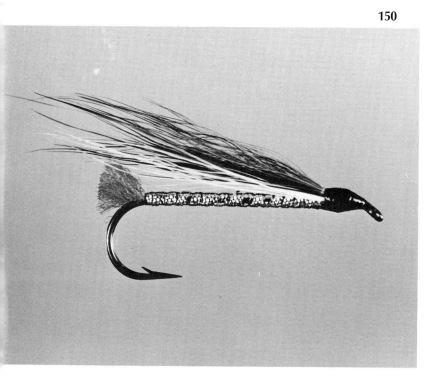

Some of the wet flies presented in Chapter Five may very well be mistaken for small bait fish rushing through a fast river or stream. In fact, they can be deliberately worked in the water to imitate minnows and the young of game fish. However, conventional wet flies are not tied specifically to imitate bait fish. There are flies, though, that are designed just for this purpose. These imitations, commonly known as bucktails and streamers, are easily recognized by their long bodies and wings made of hair or hackle. They are normally tied on 3X to 6X Long hooks; however, some of the larger sizes, such as those used for salt-water or large fresh-water game fish, are sometimes tied on regular-length or short-shanked hooks.

The Black-Nose Dace

Hook	Size 6, 4X Long
Thread	Black nymph thread or silk
Tail	Red yarn cut flush with end of hook
Body	Medium embossed silver tinsel
Wing	Natural brown bucktail over black bear over white bucktail, in equal portions
Head	Black, lacquered

Place the hook in the vise and wrap the shank with tying thread from the eye to the bend, then back to 3/16″ from the eye. Separate the three strands of a two-inch piece of red gift-wrapping yarn and tie in a single strand at the position where the tying thread is located. Make sure the free end is long enough to extend generously beyond the bend of the hook. With your fingers, hold the red yarn on top of the hook and tight toward the rear, as in Drawing **151**. Now, to bind the yarn down as a padding on the shank, wind the thread neatly down the shank to a position above the barb of the hook. Cut off the surplus yarn flush with the bend, forming a red butt, as shown in Drawing **152** Cut off the surplus in front. Wind the thread neatly back to 3/16″ from the eye. Tie in a ten-inch length of medium-width embossed silver tinsel and wind it down the shank toward the rear without overlapping.

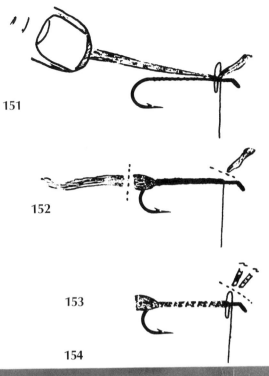

151

152

153

154

155

The last turn at the rear should cover the thread windings before the tinsel is wound back up the shank, over the first layer, to where it was tied in. Secure the end with several turns of thread and cut off the surplus ends. See Drawing **153**.

It may seem like an unnecessary effort to wrap two layers, but tying in the tinsel in front eliminates the ugly bump at the end of the body that would be caused if the tinsel were tied in at the rear.

To tie the wing, cut a thin bunch of bucktail close to the hide, leaving it full length as shown in Photo **154**. When the hair is cut from the skin it should be held in a fairly tight bunch. Keep the hair held compactly until it is secured on the hook. Remove the fuzz from the butt end. Align the tips by pulling out the long hairs and either re-laying them even with the rest or arranging them with the shortest hair closest to the hook and the other hairs graduating in length to the longest hair on top. Tie in the first bunch of bucktail about 3/16" from the eye. Hold the bunch just as you held the tail fibers when tying in the tail on a wet fly and let it project slightly beyond the red tail butt. (Measurement is for 4X Long hooks.) Take a few extra turns of thread to secure the bucktail tightly, then apply a drop of cement on the windings. Before proceeding, cut the surplus ends to a taper just short of the eye. (See Drawing **155**.) Prepare a bunch of hair from a black bear—it should be the same size as the first bunch—and tie it in as you did the white bucktail. Finish the wing by tying in the natural brown bucktail; this section should be just a bit longer than the other two sections.

To make a neat tapered head, make sure all the surplus hair is cut tapered just short of the eye, as shown in Chapter Four (Winding the Head). Wind the thread until an even taper is formed, then finish off with a whip-finishing knot. Apply a generous amount of clear cement to the head, followed by several coats of black enamel. Be sure to let each application dry before proceeding with the next.

Bigger bunches of hair are needed for large wings on salt-water flies, or where only one color bucktail is used, but otherwise the procedure is the same.

131

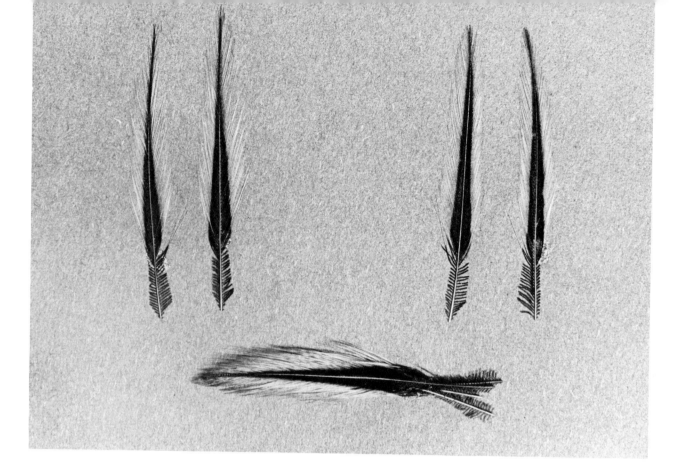

156

The Badger Streamer

Hook	Mustad size 6, 3X Long
Thread	Black nymph
Tail	Barred wood-duck flank feather
Body	Medium embossed silver tinsel
Wing	Small bunch of white bucktail with four badger hackles tied over and barred wood-duck shoulder on each side
Beard	Small bunch of white bucktail, same length as wing
Head	Black, lacquered
Eyes	White with black center

The tying procedure for this pattern is very similar to the one used for the Black Nose Dace. Start by wrapping the hook shank with black nymph thread to the bend of the hook. Prepare the tail by cutting a ¼" wide section from a black barred wood-duck flank feather and fold it in the middle lengthwise with the best side out. Tie it in at the bend, using the same method as for the tail on a wet fly, as explained in Chapter Four. The length of the tail should be half a hook length. Wind the thread forward to 3/16" from the eye and bind down the butt end of the tail in the process.

Examine the body carefully at this time. If necessary, wind some nymph thread back and forth on the shank to form a smooth, even padding for the silver body. Tie in the tinsel and wind it to the rear and back. Tie off and cut away the surplus. Tie in a small bunch of bucktail on top of the hook with the tips projecting a little beyond the hook bend. Form a throat by tying in a similar amount of hair of the same length underneath. Secure with extra turns of tying thread. Cut the butt ends to a taper just

157

short of the eye. Apply clear head cement on the windings. (See Drawing **157**.)

The wings are tied in on top of the hook with one pair of badger neck or saddle hackles on each side of the bucktail underwing. Most hackles have some natural curvature which should be taken advantage of when choosing them for streamer wings. The hackles are tied in with the shiny or best side out; therefore, the ideal curvature is that which is similar to the back half of a fish and curves inward against the bucktail. It is always best to select the wing hackles from a whole neck or saddle, for then a pair can be picked from the left and right sides of the skin to insure a uniform curvature. The length and width of the hackles depends on the size fly you are tying. To achieve the correct proportion in relation to a size-6 3X Long hook, the tip of the wing should project half a hook length beyond the bend of the hook and be half an inch wide at the base when tied in. Prepare the wing hackles you have chosen by measuring one and a half hook lengths from the tip down the stem. Hold the hackle at this point between your thumb and first finger and stroke the fibers on the lower part of the hackle down toward the butt to make them stand out from the stem. Cut those fibers away on both sides with your scissors, leaving some short stumps on the stem. Prepare all four hackles in the same manner and make sure they are all the same length, as shown in Photo **156.** Assemble the wing pairs as explained above and hold them together between your thumb and first finger with the tips even. Place them at the tie-in position, straddling the hook with the butt ends and holding them at an angle, as shown in Photo **158**. Hold them firmly and take four or five turns of thread to secure them. Cut off the surplus stem and take some extra windings of thread. I sometimes apply a little cement on the windings to affix them permanently.

To prepare the two shoulder feathers(see Photo **199** in ChapterNineteen), cut two ⅛'' strips from a black-barred wood-duck side feather and tie in one on each side with a couple of turns of thread. They should be about half a hook length long and lie parallel with the wing. After cutting off the surplus, wind a smooth, tapered head. Tie off with a whip-finishing knot and apply a generous amount of clear head cement, followed by several coats of black lacquer.

Since the Badger Streamer has painted eyes, it is extremely important to have a very smooth surface on the head before the eyes are applied. For application of the eyes, please refer to Chapter Four (Tying-Off).

The measurements used in the preceding tying instructions are for the hook sizes mentioned in the two particular dressings used and should be altered proportionately with different hook sizes.

158

BADGER STREAMER

(See instructions on page 132.)

BLACK GHOST

Hook	Sizes 8 to 12, 4X Long
Tail	Yellow hackle fibers
Body	Black floss ribbed with flat silver tinsel
Wing	Four white saddle hackles
Throat	Yellow hackle
Shoulder	Jungle cock or substitute
Head	Black, lacquered

BLACK NOSE DACE

See instructions on page 130.)

BROWN HACKLE STREAMER

Hook	Size-2 salmon hook
Tail	Yellow hackle fibers, two peacock herl tips, and two red hackle streamers the length of twice the hook gap
Body	Five sections of peacock herl butts and Coch-y-Bondhu hackle, starting at the tail with peacock butt. Front hackle a little larger than the others
Head	Red
Eyes	White with black center

COCK-A-TOUGH

(Originator: Bill Blades)

Hook	Size 4, 3X Long
Thread	Red nylon nymph thread
Tail	Red hackle fibers, topped with two tips of peacock herl, and two badger hackles length of body tied over and flared
Body	Four sections of peacock herl and badger hackles, starting at rear with peacock section. Front hackle slightly larger than the others
Head	Red nymph thread

GRAY GHOST

Hook	Sizes 4 to 12, 4X Long
Tail	None
Body	Orange floss ribbed with flat silver tinsel
Wing	Four gray hackles over small bunch of white bucktail
Throat	First a few strands of white bucktail with four strands of peacock herl about the length of wing tied under, then Golden-pheasant crest (topping) tied in front same length as shoulder feather and curving upward
Shoulder	Silver pheasant body feather, a third the wing length, with jungle cock, or substitute, on the outside
Head	Black, lacquered

EDSON LIGHT TIGER

Hook	Sizes 4 to 12, 4X Long, or low-water salmon hook
Tail	Flat gold tinsel
Body	Black-barred wood duck
Wing	Peacock herl
Throat	Yellow bucktail with short red hackle tip on top, a third the length of wing
Shoulder	Very short jungle cock or substitute
Head	Black, lacquered

ESOPUS

Hook	Sizes 4 to 12, 4X Long
Tail	Short red-dyed quill section
Body	Embossed silver tinsel
Wing	Bucktail, black over white
Shoulder	Short jungle cock or substitute
Head	Black, lacquered

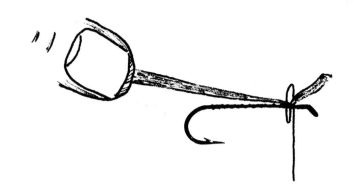

HORNBERG STREAMER

Hook	Size 8, 2X Long
Body	Silver tinsel
Wing	Two yellow hackles inside, mallard breast feathers outside and tapering to a point with the aid of a little clear cement
Shoulder	Jungle cock or substitute
Hackle	Five turns of soft grizzly hackle tied dry-fly style
Head	Black, lacquered

HOWARD SPECIAL
(Originator: Pop Howard)

Hook	Sizes 4 to 12, 4X Long
Tail	None
Body	Embossed silver tinsel
Wing	Four brown hackles
Hackle	Yellow, long and soft, tied in as a collar after wing is attached
Head	Black, lacquered

MICKEY FINN

Hook	Sizes 2 to 12, 4X Long
Tail	None
Body	Embossed silver tinsel
Wing	Three sections—yellow bucktail, over which is tied a bunch of red bucktail of the same size as the yellow, over which is tied a bunch of yellow bucktail as big as the other two together
Head	Black, lacquered

MOOSE RIVER

Hook	Sizes 2 to 6, 4X Long
Tail	None
Body	Embossed silver tinsel
Wing	White bucktail topped with six to eight strands of peacock herl
Shoulder	Golden-pheasant tippet
Head	Black, lacquered

MUDDLER MINNOW

Hook	Sizes 1 to 12, 3 or 4X Long
Tail	Section of brown mottled turkey quill
Body	Flat gold tinsel
Wing	Brown mottled turkey quill section on each side of a bunch of gray squirrel
Hackle	Natural deer hair a little longer than wing, tied in as a collar
Head	Natural deer hair, spun and trimmed

SABBETH STREAMER
(Originator: Phil Johnson)

Hook	Sizes 2 to 10, 4X Long
Tail	Amherst-pheasant tippet
Body	Flat silver tinsel
Wing	White polar bear with one white and one black saddle hackle on each side, black on the outside
Topping	Three or four strands of peacock sword
	Dyed red-hackle fibers
	Jungle cock or substitute
Head	Black, lacquered

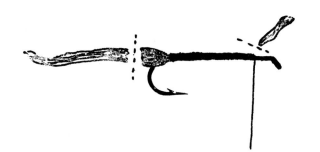

SPRUCE

(Not dressed as the original)

Hook	Sizes 2 to 10, 4X Long
Tail	Peacock sword fibers, four or five strands
Body	Rear half, red silk floss, front half, peacock herl over heavy padding
Wing	Two badger saddle hackles, divided, reaching end of tail
Hackle	Badger, fairly long and tied in after wing is attached
Head	Black, lacquered

SUNFISH

(Originated by the author)

Hook	Size 6, 4X Long
Tail	Golden pheasant topping and red hackle fibers
Body	Yellow floss palmered with dark furnace hackle
Wing	Four saddle hackles, two orange inside with one dark furnace on each side over a small bunch of mixed green, yellow, and red bucktail
Shoulder	Jungle-cock eye or substitute
Hackle	Long dark furnace
Head	Black, lacquered

SUPERVISOR

(Originator: Joe Stickney)

Hook	Size 4 low-water salmon hook (author's preference)
Tail	Short section of red wool yarn
Body	Flat silver tinsel
Wing	Four light-blue saddle hackles over small bunch of white bucktail slightly shorter than the hackles
Topping	Half dozen strands of peacock herl
Throat	Small bunch of white hackle fibers
Shoulder	Pale green hackle tips two thirds the length of wing, with jungle cock (or substitute) outside
Head	Black, lacquered

YELLOW MARIBOU

(As dressed by Tony Ottomano)

Hook	Size 2 to 12, 4X Long
Tail	Short red-wool butt
Body	Flat silver tinsel
Wing	Yellow maribou topped with four strands of peacock herl
Throat	Dyed red-hackle fibers
Head	Black, lacquered
Eyes	White with black center

16

SHAD FLIES

Going after shad with a fly rod and a handful of brightly colored flies is the favorite angling method for many fishermen up and down the coastlines when, in the early spring, shad enter rivers and streams to make their spawning runs. Many anglers refer to shad as "the poor man's salmon." Despite this slighting reference, shad offer good fishing sport for anyone.

For shad fishing, I recommend a sinking line with a 7½ foot leader tapered to .011, or about a six- or seven-pound-test tippet. Fish the fly deep and slow, and you'll catch your share of shad.

The Silver Shad
(Originated by the author)

Hook	Mustad #3406 salt-water hook, size 6 or 8
Thread	Red nymph thread
Tail	Red gift-wrapping yarn, tied as a short flared butt
Body	1/16" braided silver mylar tubing, wound as tinsel
Wing	White or yellow calf tail
Head	Red

159

160

Place the hook in the vise and attach the red nymph thread, winding it on the hook to ¼" from the eye. Prepare some red gift-wrapping yarn by separating the three strands. Cut 2" from a single strand and tie it in on top of the hook with four or five turns of thread. Let a generous portion of yarn project to the left over the bend of the hook.(See Photo **159**.) Wind the thread neatly down the shank to a position directly over the barb of the hook, tying down the yarn in the process, then cut off the surplus yarn in front close to the shank. The yarn projecting to the rear is now cut flush with the outside bend of the hook, to form a red flared butt. (See Photo **160**.)

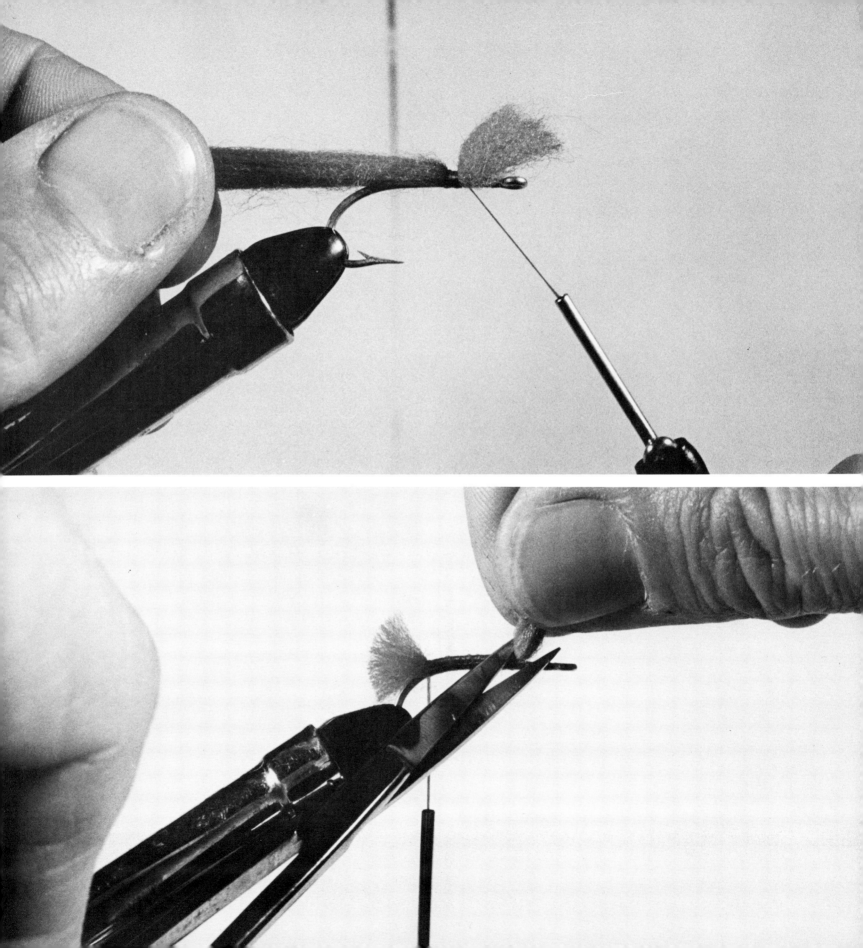

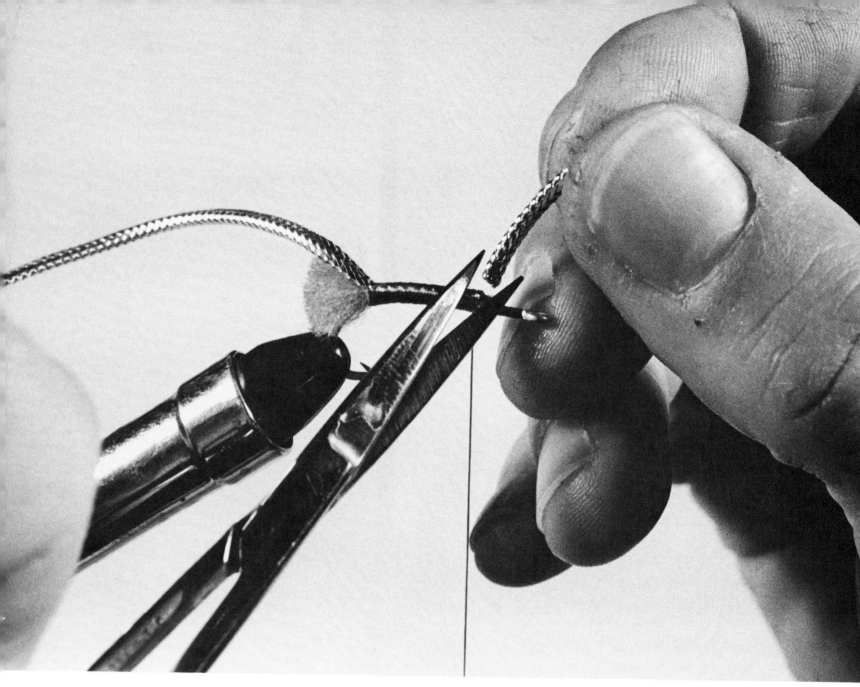

The body is made from 1/16″ silver mylar tubing with the center core removed. Flatten the tubing with your fingers and tie it in at the bend on top of the hook, leaving 1″ projecting toward the front. Tie it down on top of the hook as you wind the thread to the front, stopping at a point approximately ¼″ from the eye. Cut off the surplus mylar in front close to the shank.

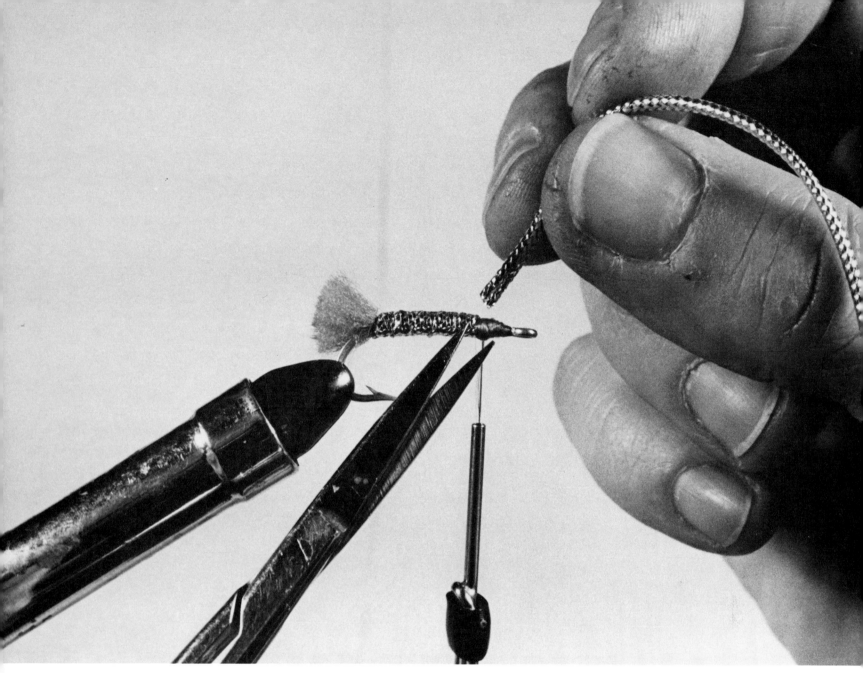

162

Wind the tubing on the shank, without overlapping, to form the body. Tie it off ¼" from the eye with several turns of thread and cut off the surplus end.

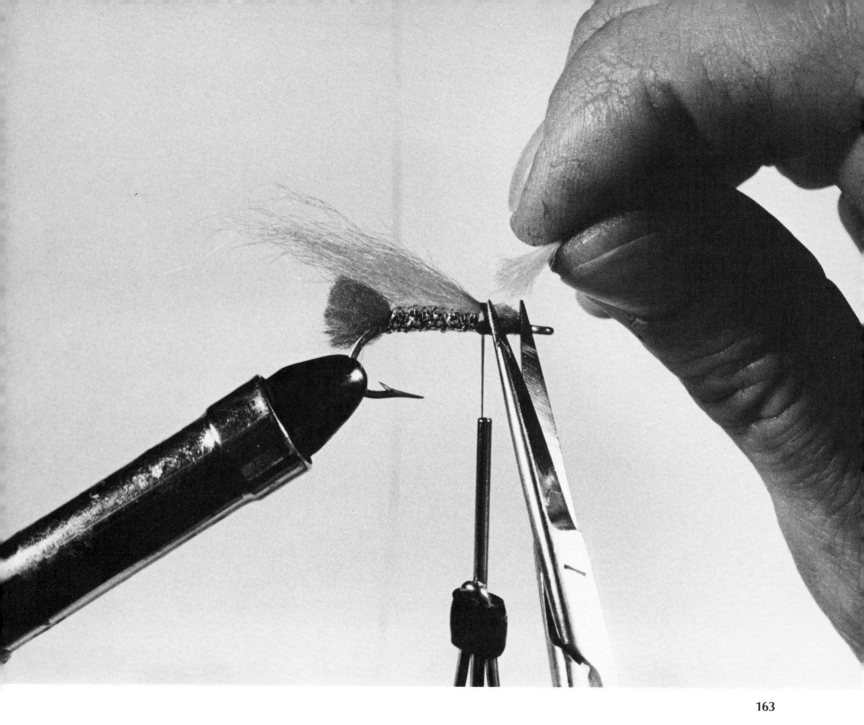

142   Form a tapered underhead, and let the thread hang by the bobbin ¼″ from the eye. Cut a bunch of hair about 1½″ long from a white impala tail and tie it in securely, letting it project a little beyond the bend of the hook. Cut the surplus to a taper in front and wind on the thread, forming a smooth, tapered head.

164

Finish off with half hitches or a whip finish, apply a generous amount of head cement, and the fly is finished. Different patterns can be tied by using other colors, but the most effective ones are a combination of silver, yellow, red, and white.

Royal Shad   The Simple One   Flidart

Additional Patterns

FLIDART

(Originator: Thos. Wm. Cooney)

Hook	Size 8, 4X Long
Tail	Yellow calf tail
Body	White floss tapered over .010'' lead wire
Ribbing	Embossed medium width silver tinsel
Wing	None
Head	Red-orange fluorescent floss

THE SIMPLE ONE

(Originator: C. Boyd Pfeiffer)

Hook	Size 8, 3X Long
Body	1/16'' braided mylar (center core removed) wound as tinsel
Tail	None
Wing	White, red, orange, yellow, or green impala, slightly longer than the hook, tied in to surround entire body

C. Boyd Pfeiffer is an expert fly angler who has created many flies for both fresh- and salt-water. Boyd also ties The Simple One on large 3/0 hooks for big salt-water gamefish.

ROYAL SHAD

(Originator: Wayne C. Grauer)

Hook	Size 8, 4X Long
Thread	6/0 nylon nymph thread
Tail	Sparse yellow calf tail, the length of one hook gap
Butt	Red-orange fluorescent chenille
Body	White floss ribbed with narrow, flat silver tinsel, with chenille collar (same as butt) at front of body
Wing	Yellow calf tail tied sparse and reaching beyond the bend to length of tail
Head	Black

Mr. Grauer also ties his fly with green or pink fluorescent butt and front body collar. All other materials are the same as in his original pattern.

17

DEER-HAIR FLIES

Many flies can be made by spinning deer hair on the hook shank and trimming it to the shapes of frogs, mice, moths, and many of the other large fly-rod lures that fresh-water gamefish find attractive. In fact, once you learn to apply the hair in the proper manner, there is practically no end to the fly patterns you can come up with. The body hair from deer, caribou, and elk provide the fly-tier with the hollow hair needed for these types of flies.

The Rat-Faced McDougal

(The Dry Fly with Two Fathers—Harry Darbee and Percy Jennings)

Hook	Size 6 or 8 dry fly salmon hook
Tail	Stiff white bucktail
Body	Creamy gray deer hair spun on the hook and clipped to shape
Wing	White calf hair or bucktail tied full, ¼" higher than the hackle
Hackle	Three pairs of bright ginger saddle hackle, stiff and fairly long
Head	Black, lacquered

When making deer-hair bodies, it's best to spin the hair on a bare hook shank; in other words, one should not attach the tying thread directly behind the hook eye but rather at the point above the barb of the hook where the tail is attached with prewaxed 6/0 tying thread. (See Drawing **167.**) When the tail is in place, apply a drop of

166

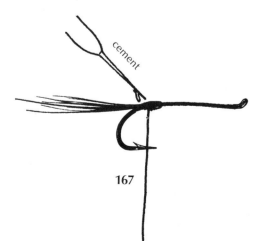

167

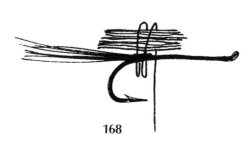

168

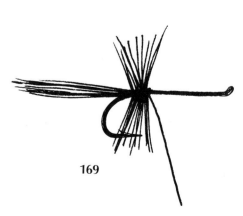

169

clear cement and attach some heavy size A or B thread over the windings. It is essential to fix the tail and windings solidly to prevent them from turning when the hair is applied.

Let the thread hang down at the tail end, select a piece of deer hide of the proper color, and cut a bunch of hair approximately ¼" in diameter. Remove the fuzz from the ends and cut the tips away, as shown in Photo **166**. Hold the hair in a compact bunch between your thumb and first finger, then place it on top of the hook with the middle of the bunch directly over the tying thread. Take two loose turns around the hair and hook shank, as shown in Drawing **168**, and slowly pull the thread up and toward you. Keep the hair held firmly between your fingers as you tighten the loops of thread. Now simultaneously draw the thread very tight and let go of the hair. This will make the hair flare out and spin around the hook, as shown in Drawing **169**. Help it around a little and release the hair in the hook gap with your dubbing needle. Hold the thread tight and straight up while brushing the hair back with your fingers. Now take two turns of thread around the shank ahead of the hair, half hitch, and push the windings back against the hair to prevent the hair from unraveling. I sometimes apply a drop of clear cement at the base of the hair and on the windings, to add a little strength.

The next bunch of hair is now added in front of the first one, using the same tying procedure. To get a compact, uniform body, each bunch added is pushed back close to the preceding one. This is done by placing the fingertips of one hand behind the body at the tail position and the fingertips of the other in front, pushing back the hair. Continue in this manner up the hook shank to 5/16" from the eye, which will give you room for the wing and hackle. Tie off the tying thread and cut it. Your fly should now appear as shown in Drawing **170** .

The next step is to shape the body by trimming the hair with a pair of good strong scissors. I usually trim the bottom portion first and then proceed with the sides and top. The trimmed body should appear as illustrated in Drawing **171**. The hair wing and hackle are now added, using the methods described in Chapter Four.

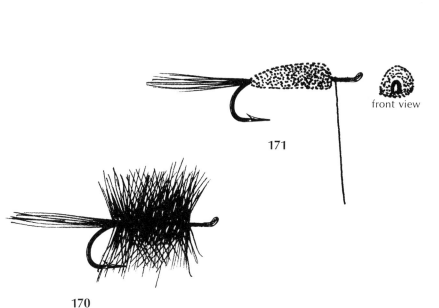

171

front view

170

172

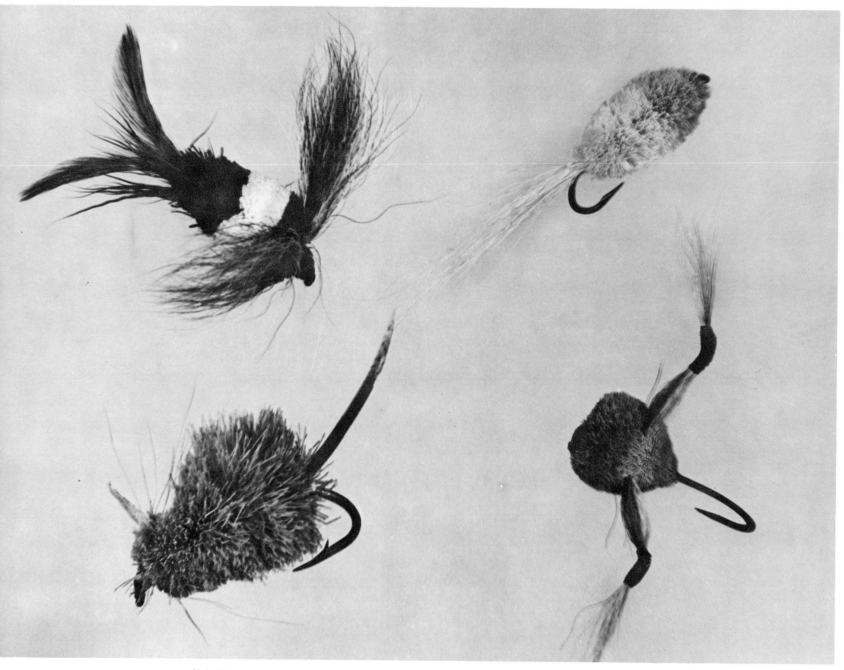

Hair Mouse　　　　　　　　　　　　　　　　　　Hair Frog

Other Patterns

The hair bugs shown in Photo **173** are constructed by spinning deer hair on the hook shank in the same manner as for the body of the McDougal, but the materials vary. The legs on the Frog are tied in when the hair for the rear third of the body has been applied. Lay two equal portions of bucktail directly on the hook shank and secure them with crisscross windings so that they project out on each side like a half-spent fly wing. When they're attached, push the construction back against the body and finish the front of the Frog.

JET BUG

Hook	Size 2, ringed-eyed
Body	Natural deer hair trimmed flat top and bottom and tapered on sides
Back, Tail, and Whiskers	Dark moose mane

BLACK AND WHITE MOTH

Hook	Size 1, Regular
Tail	Two red hackles length of hook and flared out
Body	Alternate bands of black and white deer hair trimmed to shape (round and tapered), with a few long hairs left at hook bend under tail
Wing	Black and white bucktail mixed, tied heavy, upright, and widely divided

HAIR FROG

Hook	Size 1/0, Regular
Legs	Brown bucktail over pale yellowish-green bucktail, ⅛″ in diameter, 2″ long
Leg Joints	3/16″ long piece of thin copper wire attached to bucktail in the center of legs with black tying thread, lacquered, and bent to shape
Body	Greenish-olive deer hair, half a hook-length long, trimmed round and bullet-shaped

HAIR MOUSE

Hook	Size 2/0, Regular
Tail	Narrow strip of brown mottled turkey tail, length of hook
Body	Natural-gray deer hair, trimmed to shape
Whiskers	Moose mane
Eyes	Black enamel (not shown in picture)

TOM'S FAVORITE

Hook	Size 4, 4X Long
Tail	Sparse white bucktail, one and a half times hook length
Body	Rear two-thirds white deer hair; front third, pale-yellow deer hair (trim flat on bottom, rest oval shape)

18

BALSA POPPERS

It is said that Theodore Gordon, the father of dry-fly fishing in America, used some sort of cork bug early in the 20th century. Whether it was intended to perform as a popping bug is not known. In any case, E. H. Peckinpaugh of Chattanooga, Tennessee, is credited wih introducing the cork-bodied bass bug that was the original for our modern popping bugs. Through the years the popper has risen to such fame that it is near the top of the list of fly rod surface lures for most anglers throughout the world.

Casting a popper to the edge of some lily pads, under overhanging trees, or near stumps along the lakeshore will give you plenty of action from bass and bluegills. When fishing the big salt-water poppers, just toss the lure into the middle of a school of surface-feeding stripers or blues. Don't wait, but strip in line in long fast hauls, and the fish will nail the popper almost instantly on every cast.

The construction of popping bugs is fairly simple, even for someone with little knowledge of fly tying. As head material, balsa wood has several advantages over any other material. Your local hobby shop carries a good stock of balsa in many different dimensions. This will enable you to make the heads in any size and shape you need. Other materials are rarely so readily available in a variety of sizes.

Making the Popper Head

Select a length of square balsa wood and round the four corners with medium sandpaper. It's not desirable to make the head completely round; in fact, when finished, the bottom portion will be flat. Next, sand the end of the stick to a smooth, curved taper on three sides, making the curve on top a little more pronounced than those on the sides. Continue by rounding the tip of the underside to blend with the rest. The bottom portion is left flat, but

the top portion, besides being tapered down, should also be rounded along its entire length. (See Photo **175**.)

Finish off with fine sandpaper. I suggest that you sand in only one direction—with the grain—in order to prevent roughness.

Determine the desired length of the head and mark the cut-off joint with a pencil. Place your fine-toothed X-Acto saw at a right angle across the mark, tilt the blade to the desired angle, and cut the head from the stick.

Remove the roughness from the cut by sanding the edges slightly. Hold the head with your fingers and stroke the bottom portion lightly on fine sandpaper on a flat surface.

Starting from the rear, make a hole lengthwise through the wood with a drill or a small rat-tail file. (See Photo **176**.) Bear in mind that the hook shank will be wrapped with chenille, so the hole must be about half again as large as the wire diameter of the hook you have chosen.

176

The hole must be in the middle as you look down from the top of the popper head, and just below the middle as you look at it from the side. It's necessary to have the larger portion of the head above the hook shank in order to make the "popping" effect possible. If the balsa head is to be used for a salt-water popper, enlarge the hole in the rear to accommodate the windings used for tying on the bucktail.

The head intended for a frog-type popper needs some modification. Enlarge the hole a little and make a V-shaped indentation in the rear large enough for the legs. The V should be shallow—1/16" wide and 1/8" deep.

To make the frog popper legs, tie in a good bunch of green bucktail two and a half times the length of the hook. Separate into two equal portions with criss cross windings. See photo 177.

For eyes, take two straight pins with glass heads and cut them short enough to be easily inserted. Sand two flat spots on the head where the eyes are to go, insert the pins, and apply some head cement to hold them in place. Balsa heads for poppers tied with hackle feathers and collar need no modification.

To seal the balsa wood, I give it two good coats of balsa filler, letting it dry between each coat. Sand the head lightly with fine sandpaper and finish with two or three coats of enamel. Daub on the eyes with round sticks as explained in Chapter Four (Tying Off).

177

It doesn't matter whether you paint and mark the heads before or after you mount them on the hook. However, I prefer to paint the salt-water and frog poppers before fitting the hook, so as to avoid getting paint on the other materials. With these poppers, the hackle, tails, and so forth, are tied on the hook before the head is mounted.

This is done in order to hide the bulky windings.

To finish the Frog Popper, first paint the head greenish-olive, then add yellow patches at random in any contour you wish. When these are dry, paint smaller black patches on top of the yellow, leaving narrow yellow rims. (See Photo **178**.)

178

Selecting the Hook

The use of straight-shanked hooks with a ringed eye (eye parallel to the shank), rather than the hump-shank hook used for most poppers, enables you to experiment with a wider selection of hooks. I recommend the inexpensive Mustad Sprout hook, but by all means use what you have available. Bronzed hooks will do nicely for fresh-water fishing, but the salt-water poppers must be fitted with stainless steel or tinned or nickel-plated hooks to prevent rust and corrosion. Hooking quality is often a major concern when making this type of lure. The perfect hook for a popper has a shank long enough to place the hook point directly below the back of the head when the eye is fully exposed in front. For maximum hooking efficiency, either make the head of a thickness equal to the gap of the hook or choose a hook with a gap wide enough for the size head you have in mind.

179

Tying the Hackle Popper

The first step, and by far the most important, is to prepare a good foundation for the cement to be used for fastening the balsa head on the hook shank. This is done by wrapping the shank with chenille. A section of the shank equal to the length of the head should be wrapped. Tie in the chenille in the rear, wind it forward, and tie it off in front, as shown in Photo **179** Make the diameter of the wrapped shank about the same as the hole in the balsa head. Apply a generous amount of Duco cement to the windings and let it soak into the chenille before mounting the head by pushing the hook through from the rear. (Photos **180** and **181**.) Observe that the eye of the hook is fully exposed in front and that the bend and point of the hook sit at a ninety-degree angle to the bottom portion of the head. Let the cement dry thoroughly.

If you have not yet painted the head, do it now, before any of the feathers are tied on. Remember to apply two or three coats of balsa filler first.

180

The tails generally consist of four to six hackles tied in to flare out, with two or three hackles for each wing. If you are using neck hackles, select them to get the right curvature; that is, one tail from the right side of the neck and the other from the left side. These are large neck hackles found somewhere around the upper half of the cape. You can use saddle hackles, but they lack the nice

curve of those found on a neck. Select the feathers so they are of the same length and structure.(See Photo **156** of wing hackles in Chapter Fifteen.)

After aligning the tips, cut the hackles to a length equal to one and a half times the length of the hook. It is best to cut them all at the same time to get them the exact same length. Expose about ¼" of the hackle stem at the butt

156

182

end by cutting the fibers on both sides with your scissors, leaving a little on the stem to keep the hackle from slipping when it's tied in. Attach the tying thread on the hook shank close to the popper head and wind it to a position ¼'' down the shank. Tie in the tails. Use the same method as for tying in streamer wings but with the tail tips flaring outward away from each other.

Secure them firmly with thread before tying in two neck hackles ¼'' from the head, as shown in Photo **181**. Wind them in simultaneously, using the same technique as for wet-fly hackle. Tie off and cut away the surplus stem. Wind over the butt ends and finish with half hitches or a whip finish. Give the windings a few drops of head cement, and your balsa popper is finished.

Tying the Balsa Gerbubble Bug

BALSA GERBUBBLE BUG

Hook	Size 1/0
Head	½″ balsa; 1″ long, 3/8″ high; natural with clear lacquer
Tails	Four ginger-variant hackles, flared
Hackle	Ginger variant tied wet-fly style
Whiskers	Large ginger variant, one or two on each side
Markings	Yellow with green center
	Note: This bug can be tied with any color hackle and head

The Gerbubble Bug is a crude, hairy-looking thing with a square body covered with two-toned polka dots. Don't let the looks of this one fool you. It's one of the deadliest surface lures ever devised for bass and northern pike.

As far as I know, there is no standard size for the balsa head, but it should be kept down to reasonable dimensions or it will be too difficult to cast. The usual size head is about 1″ long and 3/8″ high and cut from a ½″ square balsa stick. Sand the head to size. Make a pencil mark across the top, ¼″ from the end. From this line, taper the end down to ¼″ square. Make a hole lengthwise through the head as previously explained, and mount the head on the hook in the same manner as for the Hackle Popper.

When the cement is dry, make a pencil line lengthwise along the middle of both sides and cut a ⅛″ deep canal along the lines with your X-Acto saw. Take a piece of very fine sandpaper and double it to make a sharp edge. Insert it in the canals and sand them wide enough to accommodate the stem of a large neck hackle. The head should be primed and painted at this time, keeping the canals free of paint with a dubbing needle. When the head is completely dry, place the hook in the vise and select two

183

184

large neck hackles with long fibers. Pull off the fuzz on the butt ends up to the first usable fibers. Apply some Duco cement in the canal on the head, making sure the canal gets a good coat all the way in. Hold the hackle by the tip with one hand and gently stroke it down the stem with the other until the fibers stand out at right angles. Now grasp the butt end and hold the hackle stretched out firmly. The tip of the hackle should point toward the rear of the bug, as shown in Photo **183** . Hold it close to canal with the underside of the hackle facing you and the fibers pointing up and down. Press the middle portion of the hackle into the canal, using short movements from side to side. When the hackle stem has reached the bottom of the canal, draw it slightly forward to make all the hackle fibers point to the rear. (See Photo **184**.) Apply the whiskers on the other side in the same manner. (See Photo **185**.)

When the cement is dry, cut the hackle stems flush with the ends of the head, both front and rear.

Tie on the wings and hackle in the same manner as explained in the tying procedure for the Hackle Poppers. Daub two dots of paint on the front end of the head where you cut the hackle stems, and the Gerbubble Bug is ready for action. See Photo **186** and color plate.

I sometimes use two hackles on each side when applying the whiskers. Very effective Gerbubble Bugs can also be made with maribou feathers instead of hackle.

Weed guards are often helpful when one is fishing among lily pads and in grassy areas. They are easily put on when the popper is finished. Make two small holes about 3/16" apart, in the underside of the front of the bug. Cement two pieces of very stiff monofilament in the holes. The mono should be placed so that it points toward the rear and reaches a bit beyond and below the point of the hook.

185

186

Selected Balsa Poppers

BLACK BADGER POPPER

Hook	Size 4
Head	3/8″ balsa; ½″ long; painted black
Tails	Four badger hackles, flared
Hackle	Badger tied wet-fly style
Eyes	White with black center

BROWN AND GRAY POPPERJ
(Originated by the author)

Hook	Size 2
Head	½″ balsa; ¾″ long, ½″ high; painted with tannish-brown Plyobond and coated with clear lacquer
Tails	Four gray hackles with small bunch of red bucktail between them, half the length of the tails
Hackle	Gray, tied wet-fly style
Eyes	White with black center

Note: For night fishing, this bug can also be tied with black hackle instead of gray

BUCKTAIL FROG POPPER

Hook	Size 1/0
Head	½″ balsa; ¾″ long, ⅜″ high in middle portion; painted green
Legs	Green bucktail tied in shallow V shape
Eyes	Glass-head straight pins painted green, with white dots with black centers
Markings	Yellow patches with black centers

COCH-Y-BONDHU POPPER
(Originated by the author)

Hook	Size 2/0 (with or without weed guard)
Head	½″ balsa; 1¼″ long, ⅜″ high; painted with brown enamel which is wiped off wet, then coated with clear lacquer
Tails	Four Coch-y-Bondhu hackles, flared
Hackle	Coch-y-bondhu tied wet-fly style
Eyes	White with black centers

ORANGE AND GRIZZLY POPPER

Hook	Size 1/0
Head	½″ balsa; 1″ long, ½″ high; painted with orange enamel
Tails	Four grizzly hackles, flared
Hackle	Grizzly tied wet-fly style
Eyes	White with black centers

RED HEAD BADGER

Hook	Size 2
Head	⅜″ balsa; ¾″ long, ⅜″ high; painted with red enamel
Tails	Four badger hackles, flared
Hackle	Badger tied wet-fly style
Eyes	White with black centers

RED AND WHITE POPPER

Hook   Size 2
Head   ½″ balsa; ¾″ long, ½″ high; painted with red enamel
Tails   Four white hackles, flared
Hackle White, tied wet-fly style
Eyes   White with black centers

YELLOW AND BLACK POPPER

Hook   Size 4
Head   ⅜″ balsa; ½″ long, ⅜″ high; painted with yellow enamel
Tails   Four black hackles, flared
Hackle Black, tied wet-fly style
Eyes   Black with white centers

YELLOW FROG POPPER

Hook   Size 1/0
Head   ½″ balsa; ¾″ long, ½″ high; painted with green enamel
Tails   Four yellow hackles, flared
Hackle Yellow, tied wet-fly style
Markings Black with yellow centers

Salt-water Skipping Bugs

The tying procedure for the Salty Skipping Bugs is the same as for the Balsa Frog, but the bucktail is not divided, and stainless steel, tinned, or nickle-plated hooks are used.

Some of the patterns have a saddle hackle on each side. They are prepared in the same manner as the tails on the Hackle Popper. Also, long, slim saddle hackles are bunched and tied in, leaving some of the soft fuzz at the butt end of the hackles. Poppers with this type of wing are made up to six or seven inches long, with a dozen or more hackles used.

These poppers are by no means restricted to salt-water angling. There are times when northern pike will take Skipping Bugs and ignore any other surface lure or plug.

STRIPER SKIP-BUG

(Originated by the author)

Hook   Size 3/0, Extra Long shank, tinned
Head   ½″ balsa; 1¼″ long, ½″ high; painted with white enamel
Tails   3″ white bucktail with one medium-blue saddle hackle on each side
Eyes   Red with black centers

RED HEAD SKIPPER

(Originated by the author)

Hook   Size 3/0, Extra Long shank, tinned
Head   ⅜″ balsa; 1⅝″ long, ⅜″ high; rear two thirds painted with white enamel and front third painted with red enamel
Tail   Very pale pastel green bucktail 2½″ long
Eyes   White with black centers

19

SALMON FLIES

Most anglers who fish extensively for salmon agree that this fine sports fish can usually be teased into taking the modern-day sparsely dressed hair-wing patterns. I recently spoke to several fly fishers who are fortunate enough to fish in Norway and Iceland every year. One commented that he rarely used more than two patterns—the Grizzly King and the Professor, tied on regular loop-eyed salmon hooks in sizes 2 through 8 and dressed with white-tipped squirrel-tail wings. There are, of course, many others, and new versions appear each season.

Many of the materials used in the fully dressed patterns are variously colored strips of wing feathers from such large birds as geese, swans, condors, etc., which the fly-tier blends together to build a wing. These materials are now to some extent replaced by bucktail or polar bear that has been dyed green, red, yellow, and blue. A few strands or small bunches of each are tied in over each other to form a wing. The English have accepted this method for many years, and it stands to reason that bucktail when wet is much more "alive" than quill strips, and the flies become more maneuverable. The bodies from the original dressings have been retained, sometimes slightly reduced, leaving out only the many beautiful feathers that are no longer available.

The Lady Joan

Perhaps the best example of simplicity combined with beauty and effectiveness is the Lady Joan, a salmon fly originated by Lee Wulff for his lovely wife, Joan Salvato Wulff. If you have studied the Beginner's Tying Practice the dressing procedure is the same as for wet flies or streamers (see Chapter Four), with the few exceptions described in this chapter.

THE LADY JOAN
(As described to the author by Lee Wulff)

Hook	Usually size 4 or 6, loop-eyed salmon hook, single or double
Tag	Oval gold tinsel
Tail	None
Body	Burnt-orange wool
Ribbing	Oval gold tinsel
Hackle	Yellow, wound as a collar and tied down as a throat
Wing	Black bear under white-tipped squirrel tail
Head	Black

Start by attaching the tying thread and winding it on the shank to a point midway between the barb and the point of the hook. This procedure is important, as it will determine the correct length of the body. Select a 6" length of oval gold tinsel and remove ⅛" of tinsel from one end, exposing the center core. This small amount of tinsel can be peeled off with your fingernails and cut away with your scissors. Tie the tinsel in at the thread position under the hook shank by the core only, making sure that the first couple of turns of thread bind down the core so that it is not visible between the windings and the beginning of the gold tinsel. Wind the thread forward to a position directly above the point of the hook, then wind the tinsel on the shank with close turns, tie it off at the thread position, and let the balance of the tinsel hang down for use as ribbing later. (See Drawing **188**.) Wind the thread forward to about 3/16" from the eye and tie in a single 6" strand of wool yarn. Wind the yarn tightly on the shank back to the gold tag, then forward to the thread position and tie it off with several turns of thread. Cut off the surplus yarn and spiral the tinsel ribbing to the front, tie it off, and cut off the surplus. If this is correctly done, there should be five turns of ribbing tinsel on the body, as shown in Drawing **189**.

Now tie in and wind on a yellow hackle, wet-fly fashion, as explained in Chapter Four. As on many other salmon flies, the hackle should now be tied down as a throat under the hook shank. This is easily done by dividing the fibers on top and drawing them down on the near and far sides of the hook. Hold them in a tight bunch while taking a couple of slanted turns of thread, as illustrated in Drawing **190**.

Prepare a small bunch of hair from a black bear and tie it in so that it is the same length as the hook. Tie a similar bunch of squirrel tail of the same length over it. Cut the surplus hair to a taper in front and wind the head. Apply head cement and black lacquer for the finishing touch.

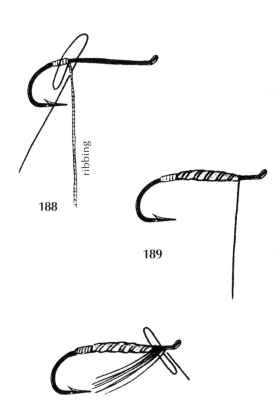

188

ribbing

189

190

163

Salmon Fly Bodies

(Instructions are for the Green Highlander)

Although I have included only reduced-type salmon flies in this book, there are certain standards in the body style that remain the same as those used in the old, fully dressed patterns.

Tags

With few exceptions, salmon flies are tied with a tag consisting of four or five turns of silver or gold tinsel, either alone or in conjunction with a small floss segment that is built up to the thickness of the tinsel and that occupies a little more space on the shank. If tinsel only is used, a few extra turns can be added to reach the position above the hook point described in tying the Lady Joan. The sketches show two desirable starting positions when making the body for salmon flies.

Tinsel and Floss Tags

Tie in a 3" length of narrow oval silver tinsel over the point of the barb and take four or five turns around the shank toward the front. Tie it off under the shank with a couple of turns of thread. Cut the surplus end ⅛" from the tie-off windings and peel the tinsel off the small stump with your fingernails. Cut away the peeled-off tinsel with your scissors and wind your tying thread over the exposed center core and bind it down under the shank as you wind the thread forward to above the hook point. Tie in a 6" length of canary-yellow floss and form the floss part of the tag by winding it back as far as the point where the tinsel starts. Carefully cover the thread

windings at this point, but do not wind over the tinsel. Wind the floss back to the starting position and continue in this manner back and forth a couple of times before tying off the floss in the forward position. Cut off the surplus floss, and you are ready to tie in the tail. See Drawing **192**

Tail

When the tag is finished, select a single topping (crest) from the head of a golden pheasant. Since you undoubtedly will need several of those beautiful yellow crest feathers for your future tying endeavors, I suggest that you obtain a whole head from the bird, which has not only the crest to select from but also the tippet feathers, which are used for tails on several of the better-known trout flies.

In length, the tail should be about one and a half times the gap of the hook. Choose a topping that is fairly straight and has a nice curve. Peel off the fuzz and excess feather at the base and flatten the stem a little with your fingernails; otherwise it is extremely difficult to keep the topping in place on top of the hook. Tie it in with a few turns of thread and apply a drop of cement. It can be moistened when being tied in.

In this particular case, a narrow strip of black-barred wood duck or mandarin feather is used in conjunction with the crest feather. It should be about half the length of the crest tail. Tie it in on top of the crest tail with a couple of turns of thread, and make sure that both materials are securely fastened. The tail is now finished. See Drawing **193**.

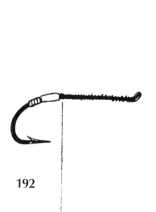

164

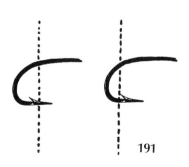

191

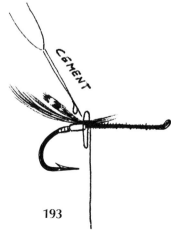

192

193

The Butt

When the tag and tail are tied in, select a long ostrich herl dyed black. The fibers on each side of the stem should be about ⅛" long and fairly even in length throughout the herl. If you closely examine the texture of the herl, you will notice that the fibers are almost flush with the stem on one side, making the stem very pronounced on the other. This is one of nature's gifts to the fly-tier, as it makes ostrich herl very easy to work with. Tie in the herl directly in front of the tag above the hook point, with the pronounced side of the stem toward the eye, securing it with a couple of turns of thread. Hold the herl straight up and stroke all the fibers to the rear, moistening your thumb and index finger while doing so and dampening the herl butt. This makes the job a little easier. When it appears as if all the fibers extend from one side of the stem, start winding the herl on the hook. Take six or seven close turns toward the front, stroking the fibers back as you take each turn, so as to avoid winding any of the fibers down. Tie off the herl and cut off the surplus. The result will be a neat butt that will do justice to any well-tied salmon fly. (See Drawing **194**)

The Body

With the tag, tail, and butt tied in as just described, tie in a 4" length of medium oval silver tinsel under the hook and let it hang down so that it is ready to be used as ribbing when the rest of the body is completed. When a particular dressing calls for a number of different materials in the body construction, each will occupy a certain portion of the hook shank. In most cases, the body lengths are calculated from approximately 3/16" from the hook eye, where the body starts, to the butt.

The body we are tying consists of ⅓" yellow floss and ⅔" green seal fur. Take your tying thread forward to one-third of the body length from the butt and tie in a 4" length of yellow floss. (See Drawing **195**) Wind a floss segment that is the same thickness as the tag, tie it off at the tie-in position, and cut off the surplus floss ends. Now select a fairly soft green hackle with the shortest fibers a bit longer than the gap of the hook and tie it in by the tip in the same manner as a wet-fly hackle. (See Drawing **196** and Chapter Four.) Let it hang toward the rear, and prepare a piece of green seal-fur dubbing, using the spinning method described in Chapter Four. Wind the dubbing on the hook toward the front, tie it off 3/16" from the eye, and cut off the surplus. Grasp the ribbing tinsel and spiral it up the body with five turns and tie it off in front. Cut off the surplus tinsel. Grasp the hackle with your hackle pliers, and hold it straight up with the shiny side facing front. Double the fibers back as you did with the ostrich herl for the butt. Wind the hackle on the body in palmer fashion, following close to the ribbing tinsel. Tie it off in front and cut off the surplus. Select a soft yellow hackle of the proper size and form a throat in exactly the same manner as explained in the tying instructions for the Lady Joan. (See finished body in Drawing **197**.)

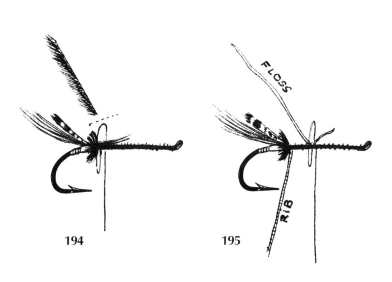

194   195

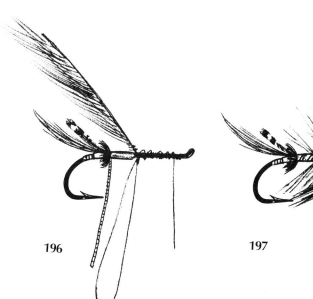

196   197

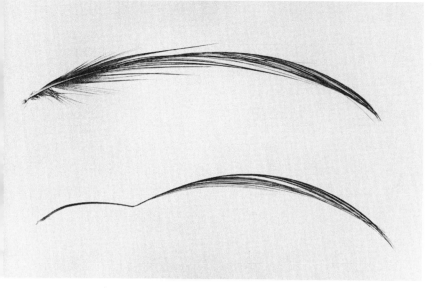

Topping

Some salmon flies are dressed with a golden-pheasant crest feather on top of the wing. This crest feather is referred to in the dressing as "topping." It is attached in front and runs along the top of the wing to the rear where it meets with the tip of the tail. When preparing the crest, pull the soft fibers and fuzz off the base and flatten the

198

199

Kingfisher
Body Feather

Same Feather
Prepared For
Tying

Segment of
White Barred
Wood Duck Flank
Feather, Prepared
As Cheek or
Shoulder

stem with your fingernails, kinking it to an angle as shown in Photo **198**. A drop of clear cement will fix it in permanent position. Select the topping to fit the size wing on the fly from a whole crest from the bird. A change in the curvatures can be accomplished by soaking them in water and placing them to dry on an object with the same curvature as the wing being dressed.

200

Shoulder Feathers

Small feathers can be tied in on each side of the fly after the wing is in place. These are referred to as the "shoulder," or cheek. Blue kingfisher body feathers, or sections of black-barred wood duck, are used for this purpose. The latter is a very acceptable substitute for the jungle-cock eye, which is no longer available. (See Photo **199**.) The approximate size of those feathers depends on the size fly being dressed, but they should be about one third to one half the wing length.

Low-Water Flies

These are merely small flies tied on large hooks of special design. (See color plate in Chapter One.) The fly is usually started by tying the tag and tail on it in the middle of the hook, as on the Blue Charm and Logie low-water flies shown in the salmon color plate. The fly is then finished in the right proportions. These flies are often used when fishing low, clear water.

By frequently consulting Chapter Four and following the preceding instructions, you will be able to tie any of the salmon patterns included in this book, and perhaps others you may find elsewhere.

167

Two English Starling body feathers, one larger than the other, superimposed and joined with a little cement to form a fine substitute for Jungle Cock eye.

Wet Salmon Fly Dressings

(*Note:* All salmon flies can be dressed on single or double hook.)

BLUE CHARM

Hook	Low-water salmon hook
Tag	Narrow oval silver tinsel
Tail	Topping
Body	Black floss ribbed with oval silver tinsel
Hackle	Blue (Silver Doctor)
Wing	Brown Mallard flank feather with narrow strip of teal breast feather on each side with topping over wing
Head	Black, lacquered

DARBEE SPATE FLY

(Originator: Harry Darbee)

Hook	Sizes 4 to 8, salmon hook
Tag	Round gold thread
Tail	Golden-pheasant topping
Body	Dark reddish-brown polar-bear wool or seal fur
Ribbing	Narrow oval gold tinsel
Hackle	Black
Wing	Brown bucktail, topping over
Shoulder	Strip of black-barred wood duck
Head	Red

GARRY

Hook	Sizes 2 to 8, salmon hook
Tag	Oval silver tinsel and yellow floss
Tail	Topping
Butt	Black ostrich herl
Body	Black silk floss ribbed with oval silver tinsel
Hackle	Guinea-hen hackle dyed blue
Wing	Bucktail, yellow over red
Head	Black

GREEN HIGHLANDER

Hook	Sizes 2/0 to 8, salmon hook
Tag	Round silver tinsel and canary floss
Tail	Topping and small strip of black-barred wood duck
Butt	Black ostrich herl
Body	Rear third, yellow floss; front two thirds, green seal fur, palmered with soft green hackle; entire body ribbed with oval silver tinsel
Hackle	Yellow, wound and tied down as a throat
Wing	White-tipped squirrel tail over small bunch of green bucktail, both materials same length
Head	Black, lacquered.

GRIZZLY KING

Hook	Sizes 2 to 8, salmon hook
Tag	Flat silver tinsel
Tail	Red wing-quill section
Body	Green floss ribbed with flat silver tinsel
Hackle	Grizzly wound as a collar and tied down as a throat
Wing	White-tipped squirrel tail
Head	Black, lacquered

HAIRY MARY

Hook	Sizes 2 to 8, salmon hook
Tag	Gold tinsel
Tail	Topping
Body	Black floss ribbed with oval gold tinsel
Hackle	Bright blue tied as a collar before wing is attached
Wing	Reddish-brown fitch or squirrel tail
Head	Black, lacquered

JOCK SCOTT

Hook	Sizes 2/0 to 8, salmon hook
Tag	Oval silver tinsel and yellow floss
Tail	Topping and Indian crow. A small red hackle point can be used as a substitute for the crow feather
Butt	Black ostrich herl
Body	Rear half, yellow floss ribbed with two or three turns of round silver tinsel, followed by a second black ostrich-herl butt; front half, black floss ribbed with oval silver tinsel and palmered with soft black hackle
Hackle	Guinea hen tied as a throat
Wing	Six to eight strands each of blue, red, and yellow bucktail, topped with narrow strips of teal flank feather and natural-brown bucktail
Shoulder	Jungle cock or substituted by blue kingfisher back feather
Head	Black, lacquered

JUNGLE HORNET

Hook	Sizes 2/0 to 6, salmon hook
Tag	Gold tinsel
Tail	Short, red breast feather from golden pheasant, with small jungle cock, or substitute, on each side
Body	Alternate bands of yellow and black chenille in two sections
Hackle	Furnace in three sections—first at the tail, second in the middle, and third, slightly larger than the other two, in front; a pair of jungle cock eyes tied in at each hackle before hackel is wound—small eye at rear, medium in the middle, and large in front (Jungle cock can be omitted or substitute used.)
Head	Black, lacquered

THE LADY JOAN

See page *162*

LOGIE

Hook	Sizes 4 to 8, low-water salmon hook
Tag	silver tinsel
Tail	Topping
Body	Claret floss ribbed with narrow oval silver tinsel
Hackle	Blue (silver doctor)
Wing	Brown Mallard flank feather with a narrow strip of tealbreast feather on each side with topping over wing
Head	Black, lacquered

PROFESSOR

Hook	Sizes 2 to 8, salmon hook
Tag	Narrow oval gold tinsel
Tail	Red hackle fibers
Body	Yellow floss ribbed with oval gold tinsel
Hackle	Brown, very soft, wound as a collar and tied down as a throat
Wing	Teal flank-feather sections over white-tipped squirrel tail
Head	Black, lacquered

RUSTY RAT

Hook	Sizes 2 to 8, salmon hook
Tag	Flat gold tinsel
Tail	Small bunch of peacock-sword herl
Body	Light orange floss rear third, with two ends of floss projecting out from body to form second tail; front two thirds, peacock herl
Hackle	Dark badger wound as a collar after wing is attached
Wing	Mixed black and white calf tail
Head	Red lacquered

SILVER GRAY

Hook	Sizes 2/0 to 8, salmon hook
Tag	Oval silver tinsel and yellow floss
Tail	Topping
Butt	Black ostrich herl
Body	Flat silver tinsel ribbed with silver oval tinsel
Hackle	Two or three turns of soft badger hackle, with light pintail as throat
Wing	Wood-duck flank feather sections over white-tipped squirrel tail
Shoulder	Jungle cock or substitute
Head	Black, lacquered

SWEEP

Hook	Sizes 6 and 8, salmon hook
Tag	Oval silver tinsel
Tail	Topping
Butt	Black ostrich herl
Body	Black floss ribbed with oval silver tinsel
Hackle	Black, soft, and quite long, wound as a collar and tied down as a throat
Wing	Black crow wing-quill sections
Shoulder	Blue kingfisher feather
Horns	Two strands of blue macaw
Head	Black, lacquered

Dry Salmon Fly Dressings

COLONEL MONEL

Hook	Size 6 or 8, salmon dry-fly hook
Tail	Stiff ginger hackle fibers
Body	Peacock herl ribbed with red floss and palmered with stiff grizzly saddle hackle
Hackle	Four stiff grizzly saddle hackles
Head	Black, lacquered

HUNT'S WASP

Hook	Size 6 or 8, salmon dry-fly hook
Tail	Very stiff red-dyed hackle fibers
Body	Black and yellow wool yarn tapered in five alternate segments, starting with black at the tail
Hackle	Six saddle hackles, wound mixed —two furnace, two grizzly, and two light badger
Head	Black, lacquered

PINK LADY PALMER

Hook	Size 6 or 8, salmon dry-fly hook
Tail	Stiff, light ginger hackle fibers
Body	Pink floss ribbed with flat gold tinsel and palmered with ginger saddle hackle
Hackle	Four very stiff light-ginger saddle hackles, faced with two chartreuse-yellow hackles at the head
Head	Black, lacquered

RAT-FACED McDOUGAL

See page 146

20

STEELHEAD FLIES

Because I live in the East, I have not had the good fortune of doing much steelhead fishing, so this selection of fly patterns for this noble sport was made by an expert—"Granny" Granstrom, of Klamath Falls, Oregon. These brightly colored flies are much like those for salmon, and the fly-tier who has familiarized himself with the contents of Chapter Four and the tying instructions for salmon flies will be able to dress these beautiful patterns without any problems.

Steelhead Patterns

ALASKA MARY ANN

Hook	Sizes 1/0 to 6, 1X to 3X Long
Tail	Red hackle fibers
Body	Cream chenille ribbed with medium flat silver tinsel
Hackle	None
Shoulder	Jungle cock or substitute
Wing	White bucktail or polar bear
Head	Black

BADGER HACKLE PEACOCK

Hook	Sizes 4 to 8, Regular or 1X Long
Tail	Red hackle fibers, with oval gold tag under and in front of tail
Body	Four to six peacock herls twisted together and wound over core of tapered green yarn
Hackle	Badger, long and soft
Head	Black

BRAD'S BRAT
(Originator: Enos Bradner)

Hook   Sizes 2/0 through 4
Tail   Orange and white bucktail
Tip   Gold tinsel
Body   Rear half, orange wool; front half, red wool
Ribbing   Gold tinsel
Hackle   Brown
Wing   Bottom third, orange bucktail; top two thirds, white bucktail

BURLAP

Hook   Sizes 2 to 8, 1X Long
Tail   Heavy bunch of brown bucktail
Body   Several twisted strands of natural burlap wound and picked out
Hackle   Gray grizzly, long and very soft
Head   Black

COMET

Hook   Sizes 1/0 through 8
Tail   Orange bucktail, longer than hook
Body   Oval silver tinsel
Hackle   Orange, long and full
Note: Sometimes tied with eyes made of silver beads from a key chain.

FALL FAVORITE

Hook   Sizes 2 through 8
Body   Oval silver tinsel
Hackle   Scarlet
Wing   Hot orange bucktail or polar-bear hair
Note: Sometimes tied with scarlet tail wisps.

GOLDEN DEMON

Hook   Sizes 4 to 8, Regular or 1X L
Tail   Golden pheasant crest plume
Body   Oval gold tinsel
Hackle   Hot orange
Wing   Brown, natural bucktail
Shoulder   Jungle cock or substitute
Head   Black

KENNEDY SPECIAL
(Originator: Mike Kennedy)

Hook   Size 4 or 6, salmon hook
Tail   Scarlet wisps
Body   Yellow wool yarn
Hackle   Palmered badger
Wing   Sparse white bucktail

ORLEANS BARBER

Hook   Sizes 4 through 8, 2XS, 1XL
Tail   Barred wood duck
Body   Red chenille
Hackle   Long grizzly
Wing   None

PURPLE PERIL

Hook   Sizes 4 through 8
Tag   Silver tinsel
Tail   Purple hackle wisps
Body   Purple floss
Ribbing   Silver tinsel
Hackle   Purple
Wing   Gray or red bucktail

SKUNK

Hook   Sizes 2 through 8
Tail   Scarlet wisps
Body   Black chenille
Ribbing Medium silver tinsel
Hackle Black
Wing   Sparse white bucktail or polar-bear hair

SKYKOMISH SUNRISE
(Originator: George McLeod)

Hook   Sizes 2 through 12
Tail   Mixed scarlet and yellow wisps
Body   Red chenille
Ribbing Flat silver tinsel
Hackle Mixed scarlet and yellow
Wing   White bucktail

THOR
(Originator: C. Jim Pray)

Hook   Sizes 2 through 8, 2XS, 1XL
Tail   Hot orange hackle fibers
Body   Red or wine chenille
Hackle Dark furnace
Wing   White bucktail or polar-bear hair

WESTERN STEELHEAD BEE (Dry)
(Originator: Roderick Haig-Brown)

Hook   Sizes 8 through 12
Tail   Fox squirrel, thick
Body   Dark brown wool, with central band of yellow wool
Wing   Fox squirrel, divided and tilted forward over hook eye
Hackle Sparse brown hen

WIND RIVER WITCH

Hook   Sizes 4 and 6
Tail   Lady Amherst tippet
Body   Fluorescent yellow-green yarn
Ribbing Gold tinsel
Hackle Black
Wing   Sparse white bucktail

21

SALT-WATER FLIES

Salt-water fly-rodding is a relatively new and exciting addition to light-tackle sport fishing. Many of the leading tackle makers have spared no efforts in providing anglers with heavier rods and lines specifically designed to handle the large flies used to entice hefty salt-water gamefish.

When selecting your tackle, remember that the fly line is what carries your fly to the fish. It is, therefore, most important to select a fly line heavy enough to handle the fly size you intend to use. A 9- or 10-weight line with a salt-water taper is capable of handling flies through 3/0. When faced with unfavorable wind conditions or when using larger flies, you may have to use even heavier lines.

In salt-water fly-rodding, the leader is of little consequence. It should be tapered, however, by knotting together three or four different diameter sections of stiff monofilament line. The tippet section should test about twelve pounds.

Salt-water flies are constructed in the same basic manner as many fresh-water streamers and bucktails. The major difference is the larger size of salt-water lures. For example, wings can range from four to seven inches in length. The flies are usually dressed on size 1 to 5/0 hooks, though smaller hooks are sometimes used.

201

Short-shanked hooks are most popular because they are lighter. Mustad O'Shaughnessy hooks are well suited for salt-water flies, and they are tinned to prevent rust and corrosion. Like most other hooks, they have rather dull points and should be sharpened with a stone or a small file to insure maximum hooking efficiency.

Tying Techniques for Wings

The fundamental tying procedures for attaching bucktail and hackle wings is explained in Chapter Fifteen. Those techniques are also used for salt-water streamers and bucktails, with the exception of the fly known as the Keys Hi-Tie. This fly, which is usually dressed on a size-2/0 Regular hook, is a very juicy looking creation consisting only of bucktail and tying thread. It got its name from its high wing, which is formed by tying long bucktail on the hook in five small bunches from the bend to the eye. The bucktail stands high off the shank even when wet. The wing can be dressed in many different combinations of white, red, green, blue, and yellow bucktail.

Start by wrapping the entire shank with nymph thread of the color called for in the pattern. Select a small bunch of bucktail and tie it in at the bend in the same way as a wing. Let it project beyond the bend approximately one and a half times the length of the hook. Cut the butt ends on an angle before winding a 3/16"-long tapered segment of tying thread in the same way you finish off the head of a streamer. Apply clear head cement. The first segment is finished. (See Photo 201.) Tie in three more segments in front of the first, using the same color bucktail and tying method. For the best appearance, try to make the bucktail on each succeeding segment a little longer than the one before. (See Photo 202.)

The top layer on most patterns is very dark—either blue, green, or some other color suitable for imitating the back of a bait fish. Interesting effects can be created by dying bucktails light pastel green, medium green, and dark green, and then tying them on in that order for the last three segments. Finish the fly with a neat tapered head before applying several coats of clear head cement and applying the eyes. The finished fly is seen in Photo 203.

Some commercial salt-water fly patterns are dressed with several long, thin strips of silver mylar mixed with the bucktail or tied on each side of it. This flashy stuff may appeal to the angler, but it makes casting difficult and noisy.

202   **203**

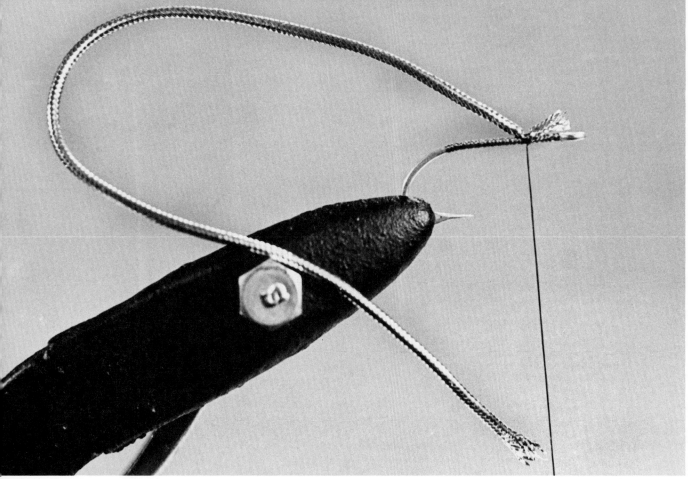

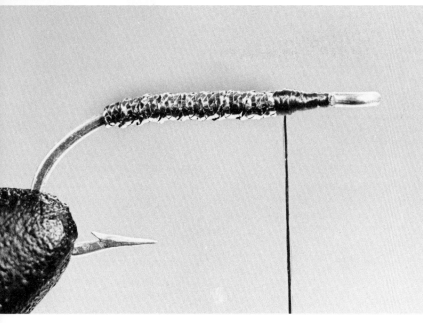

205

Tying Techniques for Bodies

The only desirable way to incorporate flashy material in salt-water fly dressings is in the form of a mylar body. The material most widely used for this purpose is braided gold or silver mylar tubing wound around the shank of the hook like tinsel. Mylar tubing is available in three sizes—1/16″, 1/8″, and 3/16″ diameter.

To form the body, remove the core from a six-to-eight-inch length of tubing, press it flat with your fingers, and tie it on the shank about ⅜″ from the eye. (See Photo **204**.) Wind tubing neatly around the hook to the left without overlapping and pull it tight after each turn. Stop where the shank bends directly above the barb, reverse direction, and wind back to the starting point. Tie off and cut off the surplus tubing, and the body is finished, as shown in Photo **205** The wing is then applied in the usual manner.

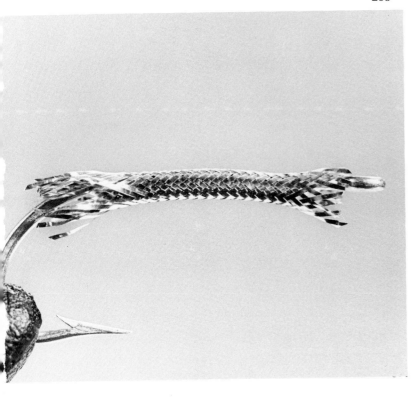
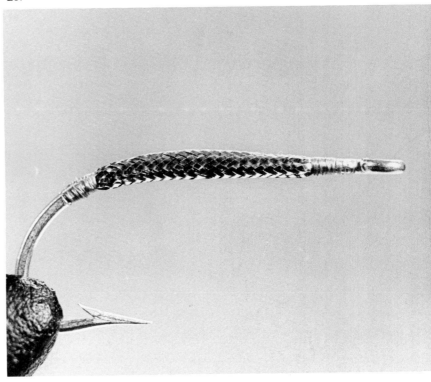

One of the simplest ways to form a body with mylar tubing is to slide a piece over the shank of the hook and secure it front and rear with tying thread and clear cement, as shown in Photos **206** and **207**. If tail is required, it should be tied in before the tubing is slid on the hook.

Mylar is also available in thin sheets that are silver on one side and gold on the other. This kind of mylar must be cut into 1/8" strips and wound as tinsel. It makes one of the smoothest bodies you'll ever see. It's specifically called for in the Blonde patterns.

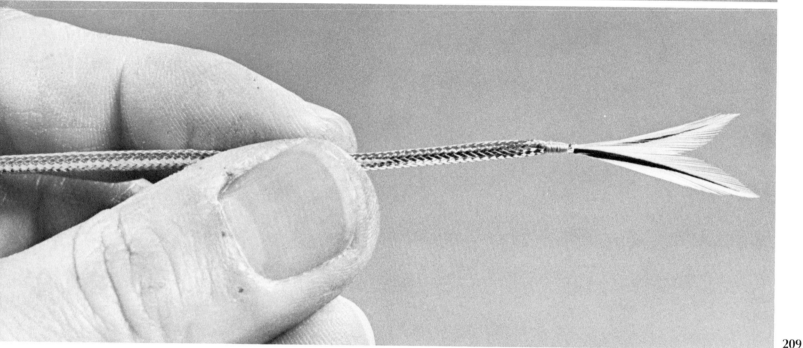

Mylar tubing can also be used as a long extension body with two hackle tips in the end to represent the tail. To prepare this type of body, cut the ends clean on a five-inch length of tubing with the core removed, and cut two three-inch neck hackles in half. With the hackle positioned so as to curve away from each other, insert the ends into the tubing, leaving an inch outside to form the tail, shown in Photo **208**. Hold the tubing between your fingers and bind the end with gray nymph thread. Pull the thread tight to secure the hackle tips and form a neat ⅛" long taper. Finally, apply clear head cement. (See Photo **209**.)

To thread the tubing on the hook, insert the hook point into the open end and push it up the tube. When the point of the hook is approximately one inch from the open end of the tubing, press the point through the tubing and push it out until the shank is horizontally positioned inside. (See Photo **210**.) Secure the end of the tubing near the eye of the hook with tying thread and clear cement. Because the wing material is rather bulky, the tie-in position is approximately ⅜" from the eye of the hook, which will leave enough room for the head. The finished body is shown in Photo **211**.

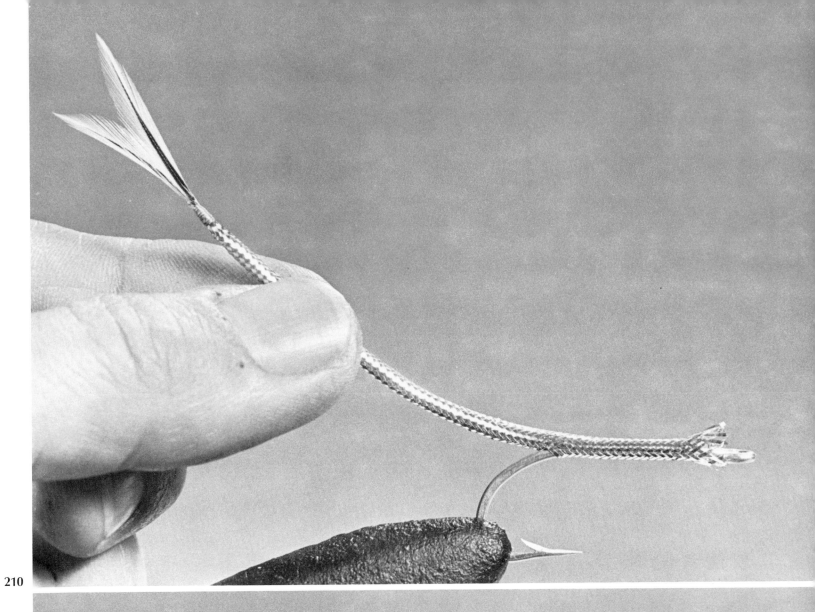

210

211

TYING THE PINK SHRIMP

Hook	Sizes 3/0 to 1 Short Shank, tinned
Body	Pink chenille
Legs	Two pink hackles, tied palmer
Back, Tail and Feelers	Natural or dyed pink bucktail
Thread	Pink nymph thread

Select two pink hackles with the longest fibers about the same length as a hook gap and a half. Prepare them like dry-fly hackles and tie them in a little down the bend with the underside facing you, securing them by the butt ends. Wind the nymph thread forward to ⅛″ from the eye and tie in a 6″ length of medium-size pink chenille, as shown in Photo **212**. Next, wind the chenille to the rear,

stopping one turn down the bend, then wind it forward to the tie-in position and tie it off. Cut off the surplus chenille and palmer the hackles simultaneously on the body and tie them off in front with several turns of thread before cutting off the surplus. (See Photo **213**.) Divide the hackle fibers on top and pull them down on each side of the body. This is best done with moistened fingers. Hold the fibers down below the hook and apply some clear cement—which will aid in keeping the hackle down—on the top and sides of the body.

213

Cut a good bunch of long bucktail and remove the fuzz and short hairs. It is important that all the fibers be long enough to project at least two hook lengths beyond the bend. Secure them in front of the body with the butt ends projecting ¼" forward over the eye, to represent the tail of your shrimp. Secure the bucktail very firmly with eight to ten turns of thread. Finish off with a whip finish or half hitches before cutting the thread, and your fly should appear as shown in Photo **214**.

Attach the tying thread on the shank at the end of the body and pull all the bucktail back toward the rear, keeping it very tight while securing it on the shank with

eight to ten windings of thread. Tie off and cut the thread before applying cement on the windings at both ends. The back should now be given a good coat of rubber cement, so the fibers will not be torn by the fish. The butt ends of hair in front, which represent the shrimp's tail, should be pressed flat with your fingers and flared like a fan, then trimmed and rounded a little like a shrimp tail.

The completed fly is shown in Photo **215**.

"Salty" flies are by no means restricted to use in ocean fishing. I have had extremely good luck with large bucktails on northern pike in Canada. I see no reason why muskies shouldn't want to try them, providing what could be the ultimate in sport fishing.

215

Selected Salt-Water Patterns

BLUE SNAPPER SPECIAL
(Originated by the author)

Hook	Size 1/0 Regular length, tinned
Tail	Very light tan bucktail, a hook length and a half long
Body	1/16" braided silver mylar tubing with center core removed, wound as tinsel
Wing	Very light tan bucktail reaching to the end of the tail
Head	Black
Eyes	White with black center

BONEFISH SPECIAL

Hook	Size 1/0 Short Shank, tinned
Tail	None
Body	Silver or gold tinsel chenille
Wing	Pink bucktail with light Plymouth Rock hackle on each side
Hackle	Pink, long and soft
Head	Red

CHESAPEAKE SILVER SIDES
(Originated by Thomas William Cooney & William Perry)

Hook	Size 1/0 Regular length, tinned
Tail	None
Body	Flat silver tinsel
Throat	White polar-bear hair or bucktail, twice the length of the hook and very sparse
Wing	White bucktail same length as throat, over which is tied a small bunch of light green bucktail, followed by dark green bucktail a little longer than the others, topped with six to eight strands of black bucktail
Sides	One strip of 1/16"-wide silver tinsel on each side along middle of the wing
Head	Black enamel

GREEN HI-TI

Hook	Size 3/0 Regular length
Thread	Red nymph thread
Tail	Small bunch of white bucktail, one and a half times the length of the hook
Wing	Five or six sections of bucktail tied in one in front of the other, each bunch a little longer than preceding—first two sections, white bucktail; following sections pale green, medium green, and dark green (top layer)
Body	Formed with the thread as the wing is built
Head	Red nymph thread coated with clear lacquer
Eyes	White with black center

Note: Many different color combinations of yellow, red, blue, purple, and pink bucktail and nymph thread are used for this fly.

PINK SHRIMP

See page **180**.

POWDER PUFF

Hook	Size 3/0 Short, tinned
Wing	Large bunch of maribou 3½" long, tied in at the hook bend
Head	White chenille, full length of shank, tied off with white nymph thread in front

Note: Other combinations of different colored maribou and chenille can be made to suit the fishing conditions.

SALTY MICKEY

Hook	Size 2/0 Regular length, tinned
Tail	None
Body	1/16" braided silver mylar tubing with center core removed, wound as tinsel
Wing	Three equal bunches of bucktail, twice as long as the hook—first, yellow; followed by red; then topped with yellow
Head	Black, lacquered
Eyes	White with black center

SAND EEL

Hook	Size 2/0 Regular Length, tinned
Tail	None
Body	Flat silver tinsel
Wing	Large bunch of peacock herl, three times the length of the hook
Throat	Six to eight white ostrich herls, same length as wing
Shoulder	Large jungle cock, or substitute, same length as hook
Head	Black, lacquered
Eyes	White with black center

SEA TROUT SPECIAL
(Originated by the author)

Hook	Size 1 Regular length, tinned
Tail	None
Body	1/16" braided silver mylar tubing with center core removed, wound as tinsel
Wing	Yellow bucktail, two and a half times the length of the hook
Hackle	Red, long and soft, tied full wet-fly style
Head	Yellow nymph thread coated with clear lacquer

SILVER FANCY
(Originated by the author)

Hook	Size 2/0 Regular length, tinned
Tail	Two badger hackles tied in the end of extension body with thin gray tying thread
Body	3/16" braided silver mylar tubing with center core removed, tied on as an extension (total length, 5")
Wing	First a bunch of white bucktail, followed by light-blue bucktail, topped with dark-blue bucktail reaching tip of tail
Shoulder	Jungle-cock body feather or suitable substitute
Head	Black, lacquered
Eyes	White with black center

STRAWBERRY BLONDE
(Originator: Joe Brooks)

Hook	3/0 Regular length, tinned
Tail	Large bunch of red bucktail
Body	1/8" strip of mylar sheet wound silver side out over bucktail ends
Wing	Large bunch of orange bucktail
Head	Black, lacquered

ADDITIONAL BLONDE PATTERNS

Platinum   White tail, silver body, and white wing

Honey   Yellow tail, gold body, and yellow wing

Pink   Pink tail, gold body, and pink wing

Black   Black tail, silver body, and black wing

Argentine   White tail, silver body, and blue wing

Katydid   White tail, silver body, and green wing

Irish   Light-green tail, silver body, and dark-green wing

Mickey Finn   Yellow tail, silver body, and yellow-over-red wing

TARPON FLY

Hook   Size 3/0 to 1/0 Short, tinned

Tail   Three red and three orange saddle hackles tied high and flared

Body   Two orange and two red saddle hackles tied palmer, intermixed and wound dry-fly style

Head   Red

    Note: Combinations of red and yellow, blue and white, and green and white are also tied to suit fishing conditions.

ABOUT THE AUTHOR Poul Jorgensen
has been tying flies professionally for over twenty years. A student and close friend of the late Bill Blades, Poul's flies have earned for him the reputation of being not only a master fly-tier, but also the foremost exponent of the artistry of blending fur, feathers, and steel into the most lifelike of nature imitations. A resident of Towson, Maryland, Poul is apt to be found anywhere in the flyfishing world demonstrating his own brand of flytying art. A Trustee of the Museum of American Fly-Fishing; active in conservation causes; and always on hand to aid the youngsters at the Brotherhood of the Jungle Cock; Poul Jorgensen is succeeding in assuring the continuance of fly-fishing in an environment beset with the problems of urbanization.

INDEX